access to history

Henry VII THIRD EDITION

access to history

Henry VII THIRD EDITION

Roger Turvey and Caroline Rogers

Hodder Murray

A MEMBER OF THE HODDER HEADLINE GROUP

The publishers would like to thank the following individuals, institutions and companies for permission to reproduce copyright illustrations in this book:
Bibliothèque Municipale, Arras, France/Bridgeman Art Library, used on page 36; Bibliothèque Nationale, Paris, France/Bridgeman Art Library, used on page 4; Bridgeman Art Library, used on pages 7, 13, 26, 30; Dr J. Burgess/Science Photo Library, used on page 121; Corpus Christi College, Oxford, UK/Bridgeman Art Library, used on page 151; © Crown Copyright, used on page 97; © Werner Forman/Corbis, used on page 166; Great Malvern Priory, photographed by David Mocatta, used on pages 90, 99; © Angelo Hornak/Corbis, used on page 165; Louvre, Paris, France/Bridgeman Art Library, used on page 34; Mary Evans Picture Library, used on pages 75, 129; Musee Conde, Chantilly, France/Bridgeman Art Library, used on page 146; The Royal Collection © 2005, Her Majesty Queen Elizabeth II, used on page 156; © Stapleton Collection/Corbis, used on page 38.
The publishers would also like to thank the following for permission to reproduce material in this book: AQA material is reproduced by permission of the Assessment and Qualification Alliance, used on pages 19, 43, 65, 88, 110, 135, 154; Cambridge University Press for an extract from *Henry VII and the English Polity* by C. Carpenter (1995), used on page 67; Cambridge University Press for an extract from *The Tudor Monarchies 1485–1603* by J. McGurk (1999), used on page 112; Edexcel Limited for extracts used on pages 46, 113, 157; Harvard University Press for an extract from *Government and Community* by J.R. Lander (1980), used on page 67; Heinemann for extracts from *The Wars of the Roses and Henry VII: England 1459–1513* by C. Pendrill (2003), used on pages 85, 109; Longman for an extract from *Late Medieval England 1399–1509* by A.J. Pollard (2000), used on page 87–8; Longman for an extract from *Tudor Britain, 1485–1603* by R. Lockyer and D. O'Sullivan (1997), used on pages 134, 156; Oxford, Cambridge and RSA (OCR) examinations for extracts used on pages 23, 114, 159.
Every effort has been made to trace all copyright holders, but if any have been inadvertently overlooked the Publishers will be pleased to make the necessary arrangements at the first opportunity.

Although every effort has been made to ensure that website addresses are correct at time of going to press, Hodder Murray cannot be held responsible for the content of any website mentioned in this book. It is sometimes possible to find a relocated web page by typing in the address of the home page for a website in the URL window of your browser.

Orders: please contact Bookpoint Ltd, 130 Milton Park, Abingdon, Oxon OX14 4SB. Telephone: (44) 01235 827720. Fax: (44) 01235 400454. Lines are open 9.00–6.00, Monday to Saturday, with a 24-hour message answering service. Visit our website at www.hoddereducation.co.uk

© Roger Turvey and Caroline Rogers 2005
Third edition published in 2005 by
Hodder Murray, an imprint of Hodder Education,
a member of the Hodder Headline Group
338 Euston Road
London NW1 3BH

Impression number	10 9 8 7 6 5 4 3 2 1
Year	2010 2009 2008 2007 2006 2005

Cover photo shows Henry VII by an anonymous artist, reproduced courtesy of the National Portrait Gallery, London
Typeset in Baskerville 10/12pt and produced by Gray Publishing, Tunbridge Wells
Printed in Malta

A catalogue record for this title is available from the British Library

ISBN-10: 0 340 88896 2
ISBN-13: 978 0 340 88896 4

Contents

Dedication

Keith Randell (1943–2002)

The *Access to History* series was conceived and developed by Keith, who created a series to 'cater for students as they are, not as we might wish them to be'. He leaves a living legacy of a series that for over 20 years has provided a trusted, stimulating and well-loved accompaniment to post-16 study. Our aim with these new editions is to continue to offer students the best possible support for their studies.

1

Ending the Wars of the Roses: Richard III and Henry Tudor

POINTS TO CONSIDER
A nation's government, security and well-being depend on the character and strength of its ruler. This was particularly true during the middle ages when kings had the power to pass laws, raise revenue and make war. However, Henry VI's weak and irresponsible rule led to civil war, while Richard III's illegal seizure of the throne caused rebellion. Richard's unpopularity encouraged claimants like Henry Tudor to challenge him for the crown. These issues are examined as six themes:

- The Wars of the Roses
- The usurpation of Richard III
- Challenges to Richard's rule: Buckingham's rebellion
- Politics and government in the reign of Richard III
- Richard III's overthrow
- Henry Tudor's claim to the throne
- The battle of Bosworth: Henry becomes king

Key dates

1455	The Wars of the Roses begin
1461	Edward IV becomes king
1470–1	Henry VI temporarily regains the throne
1471	Edward IV returns as king
1483	Edward IV dies
	Richard III seizes the throne
	Buckingham's rebellion
1485	Battle of Bosworth

1 | The Wars of the Roses

Key question
What caused the dynastic struggle known as the Wars of the Roses?

Origins of the Wars of the Roses
The **Wars of the Roses** were a **dynastic** struggle between two noble families (and their supporters) who believed that the crown of England rightfully belonged to them. The **Plantagenets** had ruled England more or less unchallenged until 1399, when some

members of the upper classes became unhappy with the **arbitrary and authoritarian rule** of Richard II. His cousin, Henry Bolingbroke, Duke of Hereford (1397) and Earl of Derby (1377), who had a distant claim to the throne, gathered enough support to win the crown for himself. Henry IV, as he became, was the son of John of Gaunt, Duke of Lancaster, himself a younger son of Edward III (see the family tree opposite).

Henry IV

Henry IV had to endure nearly 10 years of noble rebellion – led by the Percy Earls of Northumberland and Worcester – before he could feel secure on the throne. However, the most serious threat to Henry's rule came not from England but from Wales. Led by a charismatic nobleman called Owain Glyndŵr, the Welsh almost succeeded in establishing an independent Wales. With the help of a French army, the Welsh even succeeded, briefly, in invading England. It is worth noting that two brothers of Henry Tudor's grandfather, Owen, died fighting for their cousin Glyndŵr.

Henry V

Stability eventually returned to England and Wales in the last years of Henry IV's rule and a measure of his success was the undisputed accession of his eldest son, Henry V, in 1413. Henry V was a popular king and a great soldier. He had won the great victory of Agincourt against the French in 1415 and had united the two countries by his marriage to a French princess.

Henry VI

Englishmen lamented his premature death in 1422, because it left as their king a minor, the baby Henry VI. This was a dangerous time because there was no one to control the **nobility** and they might quarrel over who should rule the country. For nearly 20 years, until Henry came of age, the government of England was in the hands of a powerful group of nobles led by the young king's uncles.

England emerged from the period of **minority rule** relatively unscathed. However, when the adult Henry assumed power and took control of the government serious problems arose again. This was partly due to his bouts of mental instability but was also because his academic and saintly personality was not suited to the demands of medieval kingship. Henry was easily manipulated by ambitious nobles who banded together to form **factions**, each competing to control the king.

Confidence in Henry was further shaken with the loss of all the French lands so recently won by his father. Law and order finally disintegrated as, in desperation, men took up arms against the king and his favourites. In this unsettled climate another claimant to the throne – Richard, Duke of York (see the family tree opposite) – put himself forward. Throughout the 1450s, the two families of Lancaster and York fought for the crown. This was the beginning of the civil or dynastic wars known as the Wars of the Roses.

Key terms

Wars of the Roses
First used in the nineteenth century to describe the sequence of plots, rebellions and battles that took place between 1455 and 1485. The idea of the warring roses of Lancaster (red) and York (white) was invented by Henry VII after he seized the throne in 1485.

Dynasty
A ruling family that survives for more than a single generation.

Plantagenets
Name given to the ruling family of England at that time.

Arbitrary and authoritarian rule
The strict rule of a king who demands absolute obedience and who can make decisions without consulting anyone.

Nobility
Wealthy and powerful landowners and office holders with titles such as baron, earl, viscount, marquis and duke.

Minority rule
A period when the ruler is a child or minor.

Factions
Rival or opposing political groups led by powerful noblemen or noble families.

Lancastrians, Yorkists and Tudors

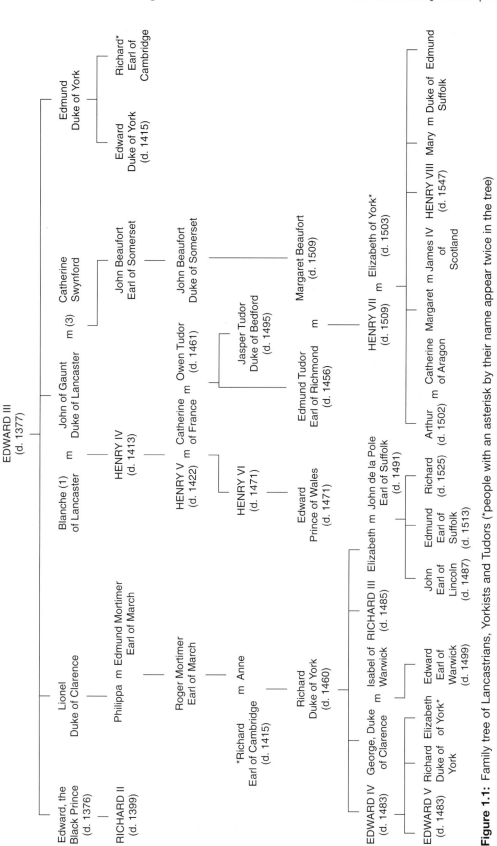

Figure 1.1: Family tree of Lancastrians, Yorkists and Tudors (*people with an asterisk by their name appear twice in the tree)

York versus Lancaster

There were three distinct phases of civil war: 1455–64, 1469–71 and 1483–7.

Key question
Why did the struggle between York and Lancaster last so long?

1455–64

What began as a political struggle for control of royal government eventually led to outright war for possession of the crown. In 1455, Richard, Duke of York, led his supporters in a successful rebellion against Henry VI. In 1459 they rebelled again and in spite of suffering a defeat at Blore Heath, they were victorious at the battle of Northampton in July 1460. Control of the government was no longer enough for York and, four months after his victory, he claimed the throne for himself. Although York was defeated and killed at the battle of Wakefield, his eldest son and heir, Edward, seized the throne and won a decisive victory at the 'bloody' battle of Towton (March 1461). This victory enabled Edward to take control of London where he was crowned king as Edward IV. Following the capture and imprisonment of Henry VI, Edward IV secured his hold on the throne.

Profile: Richard Neville, Earl of Warwick, 'the Kingmaker' 1428–71

1428	–	Born to Richard Neville, first Earl of Salisbury
c. 1447	–	Married Anne, daughter and heiress of Richard de Beauchamp, Earl of Warwick
1449	–	Succeeded to earldom of Warwick through his wife
1453	–	Joined Richard, Duke of York, when the latter claimed the regency during Henry VI's illness
1455	–	Fought with distinction on the Yorkist side at the first battle of St Albans
1458	–	Became a popular hero after his successful attack on a fleet of Spanish ships off Calais
1460	–	Fought at the battle of Northampton. Brought the captive King Henry VI to London
1461	–	Father killed in battle. Succeeds to the earldom of Salisbury. Lost control of Henry VI who was freed from captivity by Lancastrian forces. Devised and carried out plan to make Edward, Duke of York, king
1461–7	–	Became the most powerful man in the kingdom after the king, Edward IV
1469	–	Quarrelled with King Edward IV whom he briefly imprisoned. Joined Lancastrians and helped put Henry VI back on the throne
1471	–	Killed at the battle of Barnet

Richard Neville, Earl of Warwick, was a rich and powerful nobleman who used his power make Edward king. He is a good example of what historians have called an 'over-mighty' subject, because a nobleman with too much power was a threat to the king.

1469–71

Bitter rivalry between two competing Yorkist factions led to war in 1469. Edward IV's close friend and ally, Warwick, was not satisfied with the position and power the king had given him. Warwick's rebellion split the Yorkists and forced Edward to flee the kingdom and seek shelter in Holland. Warwick's attempt to govern the kingdom himself failed, so he freed Henry VI from prison and restored him to the throne in 1470. Edward returned from France with an army and defeated and killed Warwick at the battle of Barnet (April 1471). The murder of Henry VI by Edward's brother Richard, Duke of Gloucester, and the destruction of the Lancastrians at the battle of Tewkesbury

Figure 1.2: The different battles of the Wars of the Roses

(May 1471) seemed to have brought the wars to an end. Following Tewkesbury Henry VI's half-brother, Jasper Tudor, Earl of Pembroke, fled to France taking his 14-year-old nephew, Henry Tudor, with him.

1483–7

Edward IV's second reign as king (1471–83) was more successful than the first (1461–9). Once again England had a strong leader, and he strove to attain peace at home and prestige abroad. Unfortunately, he died unexpectedly in 1483, leaving his 12-year-old son as heir. Edward IV entrusted the care of his son, Edward V, and his kingdom to his brother, Richard, Duke of Gloucester, who was appointed **Lord Protector**. However, the succession was thrown into turmoil when Richard seized the throne and proclaimed himself King Richard III in June 1483. It was then that Henry Tudor emerged as a claimant to the throne. Leading an alliance of Lancastrian exiles and supporters of the **deposed** Edward V, Henry Tudor swept to victory at the battle of Bosworth in August 1485. Crowned King Henry VII, he brought the Wars of the Roses effectively to an end when he defeated a Yorkist invasion at Stoke in 1487.

Impact of the Wars of the Roses

In the past, the death and destruction caused by the Wars of the Roses has been exaggerated by historians. In reality, most of the battles (Towton excepted) were nothing more than skirmishes affecting only a small percentage of the population. The most intense period of fighting was between July 1460 and March 1461, but, as a whole, there was barely more than two years' military activity throughout the 30-year conflict. Civilian casualties and physical destruction to towns and private property were light. Even at its worst, most people were able to go about their everyday affairs.

On the other hand, as John Warren in his book *The Wars of the Roses* has pointed out, 'this is not to claim that the country was a "merrie England" of peaceful peasants and bustling towns with the occasional and rather picturesque battle to enliven the dull routine of the workaday world'. Warren claims that 'English society was marked by an undercurrent of violence and disorder' which, in the short term, the wars made worse. There was considerable political upheaval and instability (especially in 1459–61 and 1469–71) as the houses of Lancaster and York competed for the throne. There was also a strong element of noble rivalry for local dominance, especially in northern England between the Percies and the Nevilles. The nobles had seized their opportunity to take control of the provinces, so it was their orders that were obeyed rather than those of the king. If Richard III and Henry VII were to prove themselves strong kings, they would have to subdue these over-mighty subjects.

Key dates

Edward IV becomes king: 1461

Henry VI temporarily regains the crown: 1470–1

Edward IV returns as king: 1471

Edward IV dies and Richard III seizes the throne: 1483

Key terms

Lord Protector
Title sometimes given to a regent (see page 8).

Depose
To rid the kingdom of its king by forcing him to resign.

Key question
What impact did the wars have on the kingdom?

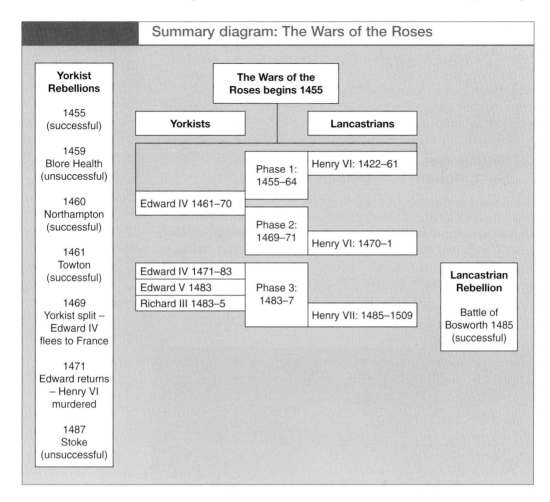

Summary diagram: The Wars of the Roses

Yorkist Rebellions			
1455 (successful)			
1459 Blore Health (unsuccessful)			
1460 Northampton (successful)			
1461 Towton (successful)			
1469 Yorkist split – Edward IV flees to France			
1471 Edward returns – Henry VI murdered			
1487 Stoke (unsuccessful)			

The Wars of the Roses begins 1455

Yorkists — Lancastrians

Phase 1: 1455–64 — Henry VI: 1422–61

Edward IV 1461–70

Phase 2: 1469–71 — Henry VI: 1470–1

Edward IV 1471–83 / Edward V 1483 / Richard III 1483–5 — Phase 3: 1483–7 — Henry VII: 1485–1509

Lancastrian Rebellion

Battle of Bosworth 1485 (successful)

2 | The Usurpation of Richard III

Key question
Why did Richard seize the throne?

Historians have long debated the reasons why Richard acted so aggressively in seizing the throne from his nephew. Having been so loyal to Edward IV throughout his reign, Richard's behaviour and actions in the months following his brother's death seem all the more puzzling. When Edward IV's brother, George, Duke of Clarence, joined the Earl of Warwick in rebellion against the crown, Richard remained loyal. He distinguished himself at the battle of Barnet in 1471, led the war against Scots in 1480 and recovered the city of Berwick from them in 1482. Richard was handsomely rewarded by Edward IV who granted him vast estates and royal offices in the north of England. However, Richard's future was put in doubt by the death of his brother because he had made enemies of the queen's family, the Woodvilles, and their supporters.

Historians remain sharply divided over the nature and cause of the **usurpation**. Some argue that it was carefully planned and skilfully executed by Richard and his chief supporter, Henry Stafford, Duke of Buckingham. Others view Richard's seizure of the throne as a haphazard sequence of ill-considered impulsive

Key term

Usurpation
Where the throne is seized without authority or in opposition to the rightful line of succession.

reactions. The most widely held view is that Richard acted on the spur of the moment to prevent the queen's family from robbing him of the position of **regent**. Richard feared that the Woodvilles might try to destroy his power by turning his nephew against him. He may even have feared assassination. Therefore, self-preservation rather than ambition is thought to be the most likely cause of the usurpation.

3 | Challenges to Richard's Rule: Buckingham's Rebellion

All was not to run smoothly for Richard. He lost much support in the aftermath of his usurpation, and court and country became disunited again. Richard's ruthless disposal of his enemies (the leader of the Woodvilles, Earl Rivers) and former allies (William, Lord Hastings) deeply divided public opinion. Earl Rivers was accused of plotting to remove Richard as Lord Protector and make his sister, the queen, regent. Hastings shared Richard's

Key term

Regent
Someone who governs the kingdom on behalf of a king.

Key question
Why did Buckingham rebel against Richard III?

Key date

Buckingham's rebellion: autumn 1483

This portrait shows a man very different from the evil and deformed hunchback described by Shakespeare.

fear and distrust of the Woodvilles so he supported the execution of Earl Rivers. He also supported Richard's regency but he would not agree to the deposition of Edward V. Hastings' refusal to support the usurpation made him a threat to Richard so he was eliminated.

Richard was encouraged by the Duke of Buckingham to dispose of Earl Rivers and Hastings and to seize the throne for himself. Buckingham was ruthlessly ambitious. He disliked the Woodvilles and was jealous of Hastings' power and influence. Edward IV had judged Buckingham to be dangerously untrustworthy so he was kept out of power. Buckingham struck up a friendship with Richard, which saw them plot the usurpation together. Buckingham was lavishly rewarded and he became the most powerful noble in the kingdom. However, within four months of Richard's coronation, this 'over-mighty' subject led a rebellion. It failed and he was executed in November 1483.

The reasons for Buckingham's rebellion are a matter for debate. For example, there has been a great deal of speculation

Profile: Richard III 1452–85

1452 – Born at Fotheringay Castle, Yorkshire. One of 11 children born to Richard, Duke of York

1470 – Accompanied his brother, Edward IV, into exile in Holland

1471 – Commanded a troop of soldiers under his brother, Edward IV, at the battle of Tewkesbury in which he is said to have killed Edward, Prince of Wales, only son of Henry VI

1478 – Married Anne Neville, daughter of 'the Kingmaker'

1482 – Led a successful military expedition against the Scots

1483 – Appointed Lord Protector of England when Edward IV dies. Edward IV entrusted the care of his sons to his brother Richard. Richard was to rule England until his nephew, Edward V, came of age. Richard proclaimed himself king after which he allegedly disposed of the princes, his nephews

1485 – Richard killed at the battle of Bosworth

Richard has gone down in history as one of the most cruel and evil rulers ever to have been crowned king of England. The man most responsible for blackening Richard's reputation was William Shakespeare. His play *Richard III*, written in the 1590s, fitted in with early Tudor propaganda encouraged by Henry VII, which sought to portray Richard as an usurper and child killer. Shakespeare claimed that Richard was responsible for the murders of Henry VI in 1471, of his brother George, Duke of Clarence in 1478 and of his nephews, 'the Princes in the Tower' in 1483. He is even credited with being responsible for the early death of his wife, Anne, through cruelty and neglect.

about the fate of the two young sons of Edward, 'the Princes in the Tower', neither of whom was seen alive again. Some have argued that their murder by Richard may have turned Buckingham against him. Others have accused Buckingham of murdering them himself. The real reason why Buckingham rebelled will probably never be known but the following may be suggested as possible causes:

- He may have been dissatisfied with the rewards and position of power given to him by Richard.
- He may have been converted to Henry Tudor's cause.
- He may have decided to take the crown for himself.

It was in this uncertain atmosphere that the distant Lancastrian claimant, Henry Tudor, decided that the time was right for him to try his hand at winning the crown of England. He had been forced to live in exile in Brittany and France for 12 years. Henry intended to support Buckingham by landing on the south coast of England, but his invasion fleet turned back to France when news came of the failure of the rebellion.

4 | Politics and Government in the Reign of Richard III

Key question
How did Richard try to stabilise his government?

The government of medieval England was in the hands of the king and whosoever he chose to advise him and to sit on his council. It was an age of personal monarchy when the king ruled in the fullest sense of the word. This meant the country prospered or stagnated depending on the ability of the ruler. In 1471, Sir John Fortescue, **Chief Justice** of the King's Bench under Henry VI, wrote *The Governance of England*, which offered Edward IV advice on how to restore political strength and stability. Fortescue identified two major problems and the means to deal with them:

- The financial weakness of the crown. To solve this problem, Fortescue advocated **retrenchment** to halt the decline in royal revenue and **re-endowment** to increase the monarchy's income.
- The increasing power of the nobility. To combat the power of the nobility, especially the 'over-mighty' subject, he advocated a code of strict discipline mixed with reward and punishment.

When Richard became king he tried to follow this advice. He sought stability by continuing the financial policies of his brother Edward IV and raised much needed revenue from the forfeited estates of people **attainted** for **treason**. This enabled Richard to grant revenues worth around £12,000 per annum as rewards for loyal service. He also tried to improve the efficiency of revenue collection in crown lands. Although he did not rule long enough to solve the financial weakness of the crown, Richard had introduced a measure of stability and efficiency in the collection of royal revenue.

Richard hoped to stabilise the government by recruiting the nobility. He won many of them over by offering financial rewards,

Key terms

Chief Justice
Chief Judge in the king's law court.

Retrenchment
Cutting down on expenditure.

Re-endowment
Re-investment, or finding other ways of raising money for the crown.

Attainder
Act of parliament registering a person's conviction for treason and declaring all his property forfeit to the king.

Treason
Betrayal of one's country and its ruler.

grants of land and important offices. Although this added to his financial problems, he thought that gaining their support was worth the risk. He relied on the likes of the Duke of Norfolk, the Earl of Huntington and the Earl of Lincoln to advise him in council and provide stability in the provinces. The execution of Buckingham showed that he was not afraid to punish nobles who betrayed him. Although most of his support came from northern lords, it is a measure of his success that no English peer declared their support for Henry Tudor until after the battle of Bosworth.

Key question
Why was Richard III overthrown?

5 | Richard III's Overthrow

Richard's overthrow was due, in the main, to the following reasons:

- Divisions among Yorkists caused by his usurpation.
- The splits caused in the Yorkist party by Richard's usurpation led to Buckingham's rebellion.
- The instability caused by former Yorkists fleeing to join Henry Tudor in exile.
- The unpopularity of Richard's policy of planting northerners in southern counties after the failure of Buckingham's rebellion. Richard's reliance on northern support turned some in the south against him.
- The rumours circulating about the fate of the princes in the Tower, the death of Richard's wife and that of his son in 1484.
- Henry Tudor's exploitation of rumours that Richard killed the princes.
- Richard had no heir.
- The growing unpopularity and mistrust of Richard even by the northern nobility.
- His failure to win the wholehearted support of the nobility (e.g. Hastings, Buckingham, Stanley and Northumberland).
- Continued opposition from the Lancastrians.
- The nature of Richard's seizure of the throne bred fear and distrust.
- Richard's rule was so short that he did not have time to firmly establish himself.

Key question
What was the basis of Henry VII's claim to the throne?

6 | Henry Tudor's Claim to the Throne

To the majority of Englishmen the battle of Bosworth on 22 August 1485 was just one more battle in the long struggle for the crown that dominated the second half of the fifteenth century. On this occasion the victor happened to be the obscure Lancastrian claimant, Henry Tudor. The 28-year-old earl was not known to his new subjects, most of whom would have believed his chances of remaining on the throne to be extremely slim. It was only victory in battle that had brought Henry to power, as his claim to the throne by inheritance was rather weak. It lay through his mother, Margaret Beaufort, who was a direct descendant of Edward III by the marriage of his third son, John of Gaunt, Duke of Lancaster, to Catherine Swynford (see the family tree in

Figure 1.1 on page 3). Their children had been born when Catherine was Gaunt's mistress and, although an act of parliament in Richard II's reign had legitimised them, a further act in Henry IV's time had excluded them from the throne.

Henry VII also inherited royal blood, although not a claim to the throne, from his father Edmund Tudor. Edmund's mother, Catherine, was a French princess who had been married to Henry V of England before she became the wife of Edmund's Welsh father, Owen Tudor. By virtue of this marriage, Edmund and his brother Jasper were the half-brothers of King Henry VI. In 1452 Henry VI raised his half-brothers to the peerage by creating Edmund Earl of Richmond and Jasper Earl of Pembroke. Therefore, Henry VII was the half-nephew of the king of England and a member of the royal family.

Early life

If we are to understand Henry's actions as king and to discover the character of the man behind the mask of kingship, it is vital to take into account the unusual circumstances of his early life. From the very beginning, his childhood was unsettled and coloured by the civil war. He was born in Pembroke Castle, Wales, on 28 January 1457, the only child of Edmund Tudor and the 14-year-old Margaret Beaufort. Henry never knew his father because he had died of disease three months before his birth.

Henry of Richmond spent his early years at Pembroke Castle with his mother and uncle, Jasper Tudor. However, in 1461, after the defeat of the Lancastrian king, Henry VI, the castle was seized by the Welsh nobleman Sir William, later Lord, Herbert. While Henry VI and his son were still alive, the young earl was not that important. He was no more than a valuable **ward** to the new Yorkist king, Edward IV. This meant that because Henry was a fatherless minor, both he and his estates were controlled by Edward, as his **feudal** lord. In 1462 Edward sold the guardianship of Henry to Lord Herbert for £1000, and transferred the **overlordship** of the Richmond lands to his own brother, the Duke of Gloucester. From this point Henry saw little or nothing of his mother. She was married again in 1464 to Henry Stafford, second son of the Duke of Buckingham and, after his death in 1471, to Thomas, Lord Stanley.

According to the chronicler Polydore Vergil, who later wrote a history of England, Henry was 'kept as prisoner, but honourably brought up' in the Herbert household at Raglan Castle in south-east Wales. The Welsh-speaking Herbert had Henry educated as a prospective son-in-law. Circumstances changed in 1469 when, defeated in battle, Herbert was executed by the Earl of Warwick, and Henry VI was briefly restored in 1470. When this temporary Lancastrian interlude ended with the deaths of Henry VI and his only child, Prince Edward, the following year, Henry, Earl of Richmond, suddenly became the main Lancastrian claimant to the throne. Recognising the vulnerable position into which fate had placed his nephew, Jasper Tudor took Henry across the Channel to safety.

Key question
How unsettled was Henry's early life and how might this have affected him?

Key terms

Wardship
A lord's duty of care for the upbringing, education and marriage of the under-age children of dead vassals, and looking after their lands until they reach adulthood.

Overlordship
One person having power over another or over his lands such as a lord over his vassal.

Feudal system
A term used to describe the political and social system of medieval England. It was developed in England by William the Conqueror after the Norman Conquest as a way of controlling his new kingdom. It was based on the relationship between lord (master) and vassal (servant): in a ceremony known as homage the vassal promised to serve his lord in war and peace in return for land. This land was held with the permission of the lord who offered his vassal support and protection. The most important lord was the king and his vassals were his nobles. The nobles were lords to their vassals, the knights.

Duchy
Name given to territory ruled over by a duke.

Years in exile

Henry remained in exile for 14 years, mostly in Brittany, an independent French **duchy**, as the guest of its ruler Duke Francis II. Polydore Vergil records that Edward IV reacted 'very grievously' to the news that 'the only imp now left of Henry VI's brood' had escaped. Edward offered a substantial reward for the return of the two fugitives. However, the Duke stood by his guests, although he did promise to guard them so that they would not escape and harm Edward. Perhaps he also realised how useful they might be in any further negotiations with England and France. At any rate, their English servants were sent home and replaced by Bretons. Edward IV had to be satisfied with that.

Later, in 1475, after he had made a favourable treaty with Louis XI of France, Edward renewed his attempt to bring Henry back to England by persuading Duke Francis that he wanted to marry Henry to one of his daughters. The Duke was in a difficult

Margaret is credited with influencing her third husband, Thomas, Lord Stanley, to support her son's claim to the throne. As the king's mother, she took an active part in planning the marriage of Henry with Elizabeth of York. She died six months after her son in 1509.

position because, had he refused, there was a risk that England and France would unite and endanger Brittany's independence.

However, Henry himself resolved the situation. Convinced that he would be going to his death if he was handed over to the English Embassy at St Malo, he fell into a fever, or pretended to, which delayed his crossing to England. One of the Duke's favourite advisers persuaded Francis that Henry's fate was indeed precarious and, while the English ambassadors were conveniently distracted, Henry was rescued and taken into sanctuary. Duke Francis renewed his promise to guard Henry, and Edward IV made no further attempt to retrieve him. Throughout this period Jasper Tudor and Henry remained in contact with Lancastrians at home, although there is no evidence that they ever challenged Edward's claim to be king.

In 1483, the situation changed when Richard, Duke of Gloucester, proclaimed himself king on the sudden death of his brother, Edward IV. Edward's two young sons suspiciously disappeared and Richard's former ally, the Duke of Buckingham, turned against him. Once again the political climate in England became unsettled. By usurping the throne and denying the succession of his nephew, Edward V, Richard had laid himself open to challenge. Henry Tudor, therefore, changed from being an obscure claimant to a secure Yorkist throne to being a potential rival to Richard III. Those dissatisfied with Richard's actions began to plot to replace him with Henry Tudor. Margaret Beaufort and Edward IV's widow, Elizabeth Woodville, were drawn into the conspiracy. They agreed that Henry should marry Edward's daughter, Elizabeth, which would help him to attract both Lancastrian and Yorkist support.

Buckingham's rebellion

However, Buckingham ruined the plan by rebelling too soon which led to his execution in November 1483. Meanwhile, Henry had set sail in mid-October, but his fleet was dispersed by a storm and he sensibly refused to land at Plymouth without the certain knowledge of support. Safely back in Brittany, he determined to maintain the loyalty of his new followers, some of whom were former Yorkists. Consequently, at a public ceremony in Rennes Cathedral on Christmas Day 1483, he solemnly swore that if he were to win the throne that was rightfully his from Richard III, he would make Elizabeth of York, the major Yorkist heiress, his queen. Henry hoped that this pledge would not only consolidate the support he already had, but also win others over to his side. It would be the first step towards a union of the two rival families who had fought for the crown for the past 30 years.

Henry's return to Brittany was soon threatened by Richard III's intervention in Breton politics. Richard took advantage of the illness of the elderly Duke Francis to put pressure on the councillors who were acting in his place to surrender Henry Tudor. Fortunately, Henry was warned in time by an English refugee, John Morton, Bishop of Ely. In a swiftly arranged plan, Henry escaped to France disguised as a servant. When Duke

Francis recovered, he was furious about what had happened and arranged for the remainder of Henry Tudor's party of English supporters, numbering about 300, to be conducted safely to their leader.

Henry prepares the invasion

Slowly, Henry began to gather an English court around him in Paris as the nobility became increasingly discontented with the actions of Richard III. After the deaths of Richard's son and heir and his queen, rumours began to spread that he intended to make his niece, Elizabeth of York, his bride, thus thwarting Henry's plan. Polydore Vergil tells us that in these circumstances Henry was 'ravished with joy' to welcome John de Vere, the Earl of Oxford, a loyal Lancastrian, to his side. Other future Tudor councillors also joined him: Edward Poynings from England, Bishop Morton from Flanders, Richard Fox, who abandoned his studies in Paris, and lesser men who had been involved in the failed rising in 1483. Thus Henry was able to plan a new invasion; the Earl of Oxford and Jasper Tudor provided the necessary military expertise, while his other supporters were a source of vital information about the conditions and sympathies of different parts of England.

7 | The Battle of Bosworth: Henry Becomes King

Key question
How did Henry achieve victory at Bosworth?

Key terms

Annex
To take over or to take control of.

Lieutenancy
An official position held by a person appointed and trusted by the king to act in his name.

The road to Bosworth

It is important to remember that Henry could never have contemplated invading England without financial assistance from abroad. Charles VIII of France was willing to provide this in the hope that it would distract Richard III from sending help to Brittany. This would enable the French to **annex** the duchy. Henry set sail from Harfleur on 1 August 1485, accompanied by between 400 and 500 loyal exiles who had joined him, and at least 1500 French soldiers. Although half the French troops lacked quality, the remainder were tough mercenaries hired to provide some military professionalism in the army's ranks.

The expedition sailed for Wales hoping for a good reception in Henry's homeland. He landed at Mill Bay near Dale in Pembrokeshire on 7 August and marched northwards along the Cardiganshire coast, turning inland through the Cambrian mountains and along the River Severn to the border with England. By 12 August Henry had won over Rhys ap Thomas, the most influential landowner in south Wales, with the promise of the **Lieutenancy** of Wales – in effect, to be the king's ruling representative in Wales – should Richard be defeated. According to one eyewitness, Thomas brought with him 'a great band of soldiers' some 800 strong. From north Wales Henry was joined by William ap Gruffudd who led the largest of several contingents totalling some 500 men.

Henry reached Shrewsbury on 15 August with an army swollen to around 5000 men, mainly Welsh recruits, but could not hope to win a battle unless he obtained more support from the English nobility. Henry's main hope lay with two brothers – his stepfather, Lord Stanley, and Sir William Stanley – whose lands included much of north Wales, Cheshire and the Borders. They sent money, but did so secretly as Richard held Lord Stanley's eldest son as hostage for his father's good behaviour. However, Henry was confident enough of their support to march further into England, gaining the additional support of Gilbert Talbot, the powerful uncle of the Earl of Shrewsbury, and 500 of his men.

The battle of Bosworth

Richard was in residence at Nottingham Castle when he learnt of the invasion. He did not act immediately because he thought that his rival would be defeated in Wales by either Rhys ap Thomas in the south, or the Stanleys in the north. When he realised his mistake, he moved his troops to Leicester. The two armies confronted each other just outside the small village of Market Bosworth in Leicestershire on 22 August. Henry's forces now numbered between 5000 and 6000 men, Richard's forces outnumbering them two to one. The records do not make clear whether or not this included the Stanleys' force of 3000, which remained on the sidelines for most of the battle. Neither Richard nor Henry knew for certain on whose side the notoriously unreliable Stanleys intended to intervene.

> **Key date**
> Battle of Bosworth: 22 August 1485

The majority of the recruits to Henry's army were not professional soldiers but they had probably seen some active service during the civil wars. For the most part they were tenant farmers recruited by their landlords to serve for a limited period. They were lightly armed and tended to fill the ranks as archers and spearmen. The more professional troops or **retainers** and mercenaries fought as men-at-arms, with sword, shield and pike. The landowners, the majority of whom were nobles, knights and squires, wore armour and fought on horseback. They were the cavalry which provided Henry's army with the necessary mobility on the battlefield. Henry relied on the military expertise of his uncle Jasper and the Earl of Oxford to guide him in battle.

> **Key term**
> **Retainers**
> A small, permanent professional force of trained soldiers who wore the uniform of the lords they served either for pay or for land.

Since England had no regular standing army, Richard's troops were probably similar in quality and background to those of his enemy.

- Richard's troops were better equipped and he had considerably more cavalry than Henry.
- Richard's army had come a shorter distance so were fresher than Henry's troops, who had had a fortnight's hard marching.
- What artillery Henry had been able to bring with him could only have consisted of light field guns, certainly inferior to the heavier artillery available to Richard's army.
- Richard had vastly more experience of warfare and military command than Henry and he had had ample time to prepare his defences. This enabled him to occupy the more favourable tactical position on the battlefield, the high ground on Ambion Hill with marshland protecting the flank.

Profile: Jasper Tudor 1431–95

c. 1431	– Second son born to Owen Tudor, a Welsh squire in the service of the Royal Household and Queen Catherine of France, the widow of King Henry V
1452	– Created Earl of Pembroke by his half-brother King Henry VI
1457–61	– Ruled south Wales on behalf of King Henry VI
1461	– Fled into exile after defeat in the battle of Mortimer's Cross
1462	– Deprived of his earldom and title
1470–1	– Restored to power during Henry VI's brief second reign
1471	– Fled for a third time into exile after the Lancastrian defeat at the battle of Tewkesbury taking his nephew, Henry, with him
1471–85	– Spent the next 14 years in France bringing up and protecting his nephew from various Yorkist plots intended to murder him
1485	– After victory in the battle of Bosworth he was restored to his Earldom of Pembroke and created Duke of Bedford
1495	– After 10 years' loyal service on the King's Council Jasper died childless

Jasper Tudor did much to influence the way in which Henry VII ruled the kingdom. He was the first one to whom the young and inexperienced king turned to for advice. He was a permanent member of the King's Council and his appointment to positions of power in Wales and Ireland kept these distant parts of the realm under firm royal control.

No eyewitness account of the battle exists but, by piecing together later accounts, we learn that fighting began early in the morning with Henry's forces charging across a marshy area towards the king's army. The battle only lasted about three hours, but was bitterly contested with heavy casualties on both sides. According to Polydore Vergil, Henry fought bravely and 'bore the brunt longer than his own soldiers … who were almost out of hope of victory'. The turning point came when Richard suddenly decided to strike at Henry himself. Having spotted Henry riding towards the Stanleys in the company of a relatively small band of men, Richard, accompanied by no more than 100 men, launched a furious assault on him. He almost succeeded, slaughtering Henry's standard-bearer before his personal guard closed ranks.

At this crucial moment Henry's step-uncle, Sir William Stanley, waiting in the wings to see the direction in which the battle would go, rushed to his rescue. Stanley's cavalry, perhaps some 500 strong, overwhelmed Richard who refused to quit the battlefield. Richard's death concluded the battle and the leaderless Yorkists fled. According to Vergil, Lord Stanley himself picked up the crown from 'the spoils of battle' and placed it on Henry Tudor's head. Richard's naked body was tossed over a mule and taken to Leicester to be buried. The long years in exile were over for Henry.

Bosworth was, arguably, the final act in the civil conflict known as the Wars of the Roses, which had dominated England's political, social and economic life throughout the fifteenth century. For this reason 1485 is often seen as a watershed in the history of England. It is a date frequently used as a division between what historians call the medieval and the early modern periods. The reign of Henry VII ended the civil war and heralded the foundation of a new dynasty, the Tudors.

Summary diagram: Henry becomes king

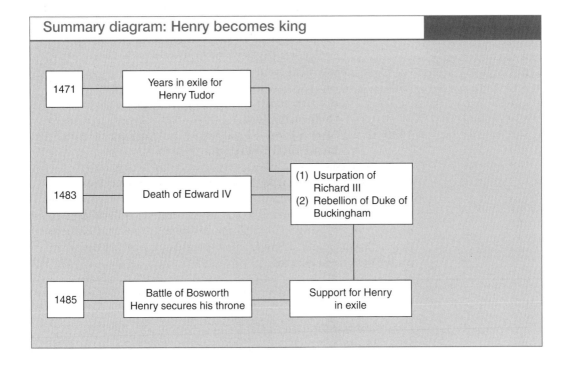

Study Guide: AS Questions

In the style of AQA
Read the following source and then answer the questions that follow.

Adapted from: Philip Edwards, The Making of the Modern English State, 1460–1660, *2001.*

Henry Tudor's chances came with the division of the Yorkists caused by Richard III's usurpation of the throne in 1483. In Brittany, and then in France, Henry could pose as an alternative king of England. The discontented certainly did assemble under his banner in exile.

(a) Comment on 'usurpation' in the context of 1483.

(3 marks)

(b) Explain why Richard III's position as king was unstable in the years 1483 to 1485. (7 marks)

Source: AQA, 2003

(c) To what extent can Richard III be blamed for his overthrow by Henry Tudor? (15 marks)

Exam tips

The cross-references are intended to take you straight to the material that will help you to answer the questions.

1. In question **(a)** you should provide a developed explanation demonstrating understanding of the issue of usurpation linked to the context, for example:
   - Richard was fearful of his own security because his disposal of the Woodvilles and Lord Hastings had split the Yorkist party (pages 8–9).
   - Richard felt he had no choice but to replace his nephew Edward V with himself (pages 7–8).
   - Richard justified his usurpation by claiming that his nephews were illegitimate, which made him heir to the throne (pages 8–9).

2. In question **(b)** you have to demonstrate a confident understanding of a range of factors, make links and draw conclusions to show why Richard's position as king was unstable, for example:
   - The splits caused in the Yorkist party by Richard's usurpation led to Buckingham's rebellion (pages 8–9).
   - The instability caused by former Yorkists fleeing to join Henry Tudor in exile (pages 10–11).
   - The unpopularity of Richard's policy of planting northerners in southern counties after the failure of Buckingham's rebellion (page 11).
   - The rumours circulating about the fate of the princes in the Tower, the death of Richard's wife and that of his son in 1484 (pages 10–11).

3. In question **(c)** the key element is why Richard III was overthrown by Henry Tudor and whether or not he was to blame, for example:
   - You must try to make effective use of the source by first understanding and then explaining what it is saying. For example, it suggests that Richard's overthrow was due to the divisions among Yorkists caused by his usurpation.
   - You should provide a range of reasons in addition to the one suggested by the source. For example, Henry Tudor's exploitation of rumours that Richard killed the princes, the fact Richard had no heir, the growing unpopularity and mistrust of Richard even by the northern nobility (see page 8).
   - You should be able to come to a judgement on whether Henry's overthrow of Richard was due to his actions or to the actions of others (pages 11–18).

In the style of Edexcel

Study Sources 1–5 below and answer questions (a)–(d) that follow.

Source 1

From: Philippe de Commines, Memoirs: The Reign of Louis XI 1461–83, *written in the French court in the 1490s.*

God suddenly raised up against King Richard an enemy who had neither money, nor rights, so I believe, to the Crown of England, nor any reputation except what his own person and honesty brought him. He crossed over to Wales and after three or four days he encountered cruel King Richard. He was killed on the battlefield. Henry was crowned king and he is still ruling today.

Source 2

From: Polydore Vergil, History of England, *written in 1513.*

At the Battle of Bosworth the number of Henry Tudor's soldiers, altogether, was scarcely 5000 … The king's forces were twice as many and more.

Henry bore the brunt of the fighting longer than even his own soldiers would have thought, who were now almost out of hope of victory, when … truly in a very moment [the king's forces] fled, and King Richard alone was killed fighting manfully in the thickest press of his enemies.

Source 3

From: Edward Hall, Union of the Noble and Illustre Famelies of Lancastre and York, *written in 1542. Part of Henry Tudor's address to his troops on the eve of the battle of Bosworth.*

We have without resistance penetrated the ample region and large country of Wales … If we had come to conquer Wales and achieved it, our praise had been great and our gain more; but if we win this battle, the whole rich realm of England shall be ours, the profit shall be ours and the honour ours.

Source 4

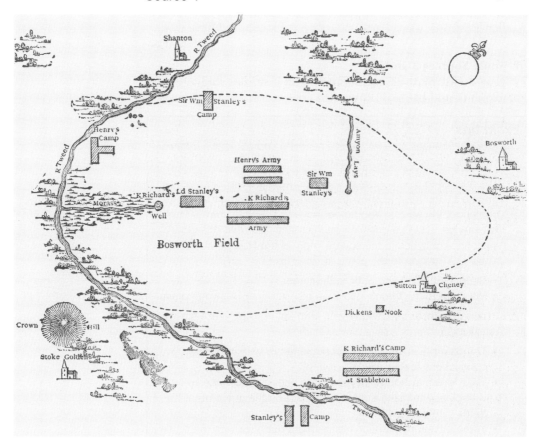

A plan showing the location of the opposing forces at the battle of Bosworth. The plan was drawn some years later.

Source 5

From: Sir Glanmor Williams, Henry Tudor and Wales, *published in 1985.*

On paper, the odds favoured Richard beforehand. Bosworth was a battle that perhaps he should have won; but the result was no foregone conclusion. The men of the fifteenth century firmly believed that the outcome of every battle lay in the hands of God.

(a) Study Source 1
   What can you learn from Source 1 about Henry Tudor's claim to the throne of England? (6 marks)

(b) Use your own knowledge
   Use your own knowledge to explain the significance of the Stanleys' contribution to Henry's victory at Bosworth.
   (10 marks)

(c) Study Sources 2 and 5

How far does Source 2 support the view expressed in Source 5
that Bosworth was a battle that Richard III should have won?

(10 marks)

(d) Study Sources 3 and 4

How useful are these two sources to an historian studying the
march to and battle of Bosworth? (10 marks)

Exam tips

*The cross-references are intended to take you straight to the material
that will help you to answer the questions.*

1. The answer to question **(a)** is to be found entirely within
   Source 1. You have to show that you have understood the
   content of the source. You do not have to use your own
   knowledge. This is a question on inference, i.e. what does the
   evidence contained in the source imply about Henry's claim?
   Keep your answer to the point, for example:

   - Henry had little or no right to the throne.
   - His claim to the throne rested on his victory at Bosworth alone.

2. In question **(b)** you must use your own knowledge to explain the
   reference to 'the Stanleys', for example:

   - The Stanleys were a powerful noble family with important
     connections (pages 16–17).
   - Their forces at Bosworth were large enough and sufficiently
     well-placed to make a decisive impact on the outcome of the
     battle (see pages 16–17).
   - Without their intervention Henry might not have won the battle
     (page 17).

3. In question **(c)** you have to understand what is being said in
   Sources 2 and 5 and evaluate and explain the extent to which
   the sources agree. For example, Source 2 suggests that Richard
   should have won because:

   - his forces greatly outnumbered Henry's
   - his reckless tactics may have been at fault
   - the fighting spirit of his troops may have been lacking.

4. In question **(d)** you must evaluate the utility of the sources. How
   useful would these sources be to an historian studying the march
   to and battle of Bosworth? The 'How useful' formula requires you
   to assess a source by exploring the ways in which it can
   contribute to an enquiry. This depends not only on what
   information it contains, but also on its nature and origin, i.e. who
   said it and why? For example:

   - At the very least the sources are useful because they discuss
     the march to and battle of Bosworth.
   - They seem to have been compiled with the aid of eye-witness
     testimony.
   - On the other hand, they were compiled years later during the
     reign of later Tudor monarchs, so they might be biased and
     unreliable. Why did Hall write what he did and how accurate
     was he? Can he be trusted?

In the style of OCR

(a) Why did Henry Tudor win the battle of Bosworth?

(45 marks)

(b) Assess the view that the *most* important reason for the overthrow of Richard III was his failure to maintain the loyalty of the nobility.

(45 marks)

Source: OCR, 2003

Exam tips

The cross-references are intended to take you straight to the material which will help you to answer the questions.

1. In question **(a)** you should focus on and explain the reasons for Henry Tudor's victory at Bosworth (pages 16–18).

   You should note that 'explain' does not mean producing a descriptive list of causes – that will result in a low mark. What is needed is an answer that offers assessment and evaluation from start to finish, for example:

   - Henry's courage and leadership in battle.
   - The generalship of his commanders, e.g. Earl of Oxford and Jasper Tudor.
   - The military intervention of the Stanleys.

   To balance this, you should aim to discuss the following to show that events and actions beyond Henry's control also played a significant part in his victory, for example:

   - The luke-warm efforts of some of Richard's noble supporters, e.g. Earl of Northumberland.
   - Richard's courageous but futile attempt to kill Henry Tudor.

2. In question **(b)** you should focus on and explain the reasons for the fall of a controversial ruler.

   You must adopt an analytical rather than a narrative approach to answering this question, e.g. you must compare and evaluate the reason mentioned (loyalty of the nobility) in the question with other equally relevant reasons rather than simply offer a descriptive list of causes. The question is correct to say that Richard failed to win the wholehearted support of the nobility (e.g. Hastings, Buckingham, Stanley and Northumberland) but there were other factors, for example:

   - Continued opposition from the Lancastrians (page 9).
   - The nature of Richard's seizure of the throne bred fear and distrust (pages 8–9).
   - Richard's rule was so short that he did not have time to firmly establish himself (page 11).
   - Richard's reliance on northern support turned some in the south against him (page 11).

2 Securing the Throne: Threats to the Dynasty

POINTS TO CONSIDER

Winning the battle of Bosworth secured Henry the throne, but it did not give him security. Henry faced a number of challenges to his rule but the most dangerous centred around the pretenders – Lambert Simnel and Perkin Warbeck – and their Yorkist supporters. The threats to the Tudor dynasty and the means by which Henry VII secured his throne are examined as six themes:

- Aims and character of the new king
- The search for security
- Challenges to Henry's rule: pretenders and protests
- The threat posed by Lambert Simnel 1486–7
- Perkin Warbeck 1491–9
- Further Yorkist threats 1499–1506

Key dates

1485	Henry crowned as King Henry VII
1486	Marriage of Henry and Elizabeth of York
	Birth of a son and heir, Arthur
1487	Simnel's rebellion and the battle of Stoke
1489	Rebellion in Yorkshire
1491–9	Warbeck's rebellion
1497	Rebellion in Cornwall
1499	Warbeck and the Earl of Warwick executed

1 | Aims and Character of the New King

Aims

> We will unite the white rose and the red:
> Smile, heaven, upon this fair conjunction
> That long hath frowned upon their enmity!
> All this divided York and Lancaster …
> Now civil wounds are stopped, peace lives again:
> That she may long live here, God say Amen!

Key question
What were Henry's main aims for his reign?

These were the words that William Shakespeare, writing about a century after the events he was describing, chose to place into the mouth of Henry VII at the moment he became king. They reflect the typical late sixteenth century Englishman's view of the nature of the achievements of the founder of his country's current dynasty. Henry Tudor was seen as the monarch who brought the turmoil of the recent civil war to an end, uniting the rival houses of Lancaster and York.

If Henry VII had been able to speak for himself it is likely that he would have identified one essential aim: to remain king and hand on an unchallenged succession to his descendants. His policies at home and abroad were dictated by this aim. Therefore, his goals were simple: to secure and strengthen his dynasty. He knew that if he was to prove himself a strong king and maintain full control of his realm he would have to establish effective government, maintain law and order, control the nobility and secure the crown's finances. He would also need good advice, friends abroad and a considerable amount of luck.

Key question
What was Henry Tudor like?

Character

The character and personality of Henry VII remain shadowy and elusive today, just as it was to his own subjects in 1485. There is less evidence about him than about any other of the Tudors. He emerges from history books as a rather dull character, in stark contrast to the vivid and lively personalities of his son, Henry VIII, and his granddaughter, Elizabeth I, about whom contemporaries wrote at great length.

However, the uncertainty about the personality of the first Tudor monarch is a good example of how limited evidence can lead to widely differing opinions. Historians tend to disagree about Henry's character, mainly because kings rarely recorded their own thoughts, with the result that people have had to draw their own conclusions from his actions and policies.

However, some of the views of his contemporaries have survived. Among the more interesting, if not necessarily the most useful, is the portrait of Henry VII (closely resembling the portrait on the front cover of this book) by Sittow, a talented artist of the northern **Renaissance** in Flanders. It was painted at an actual sitting in 1505. The following brief description is by Polydore Vergil, a brilliant Italian scholar who arrived at the English court in 1501. Henry was so impressed by Vergil's understanding of history that he urged him to write a history of England. This is his description of Henry in his *Anglica Historia*:

Key term

Renaissance
A rebirth of learning and the arts, which encouraged writers and artists to become part of what was called the spirit of new learning.

> His appearance was remarkably attractive and his face was cheerful, especially when speaking; his eyes were small and blue, his teeth few, poor and blackish; his hair was thin and white; his complexion sallow.

It is useful to compare Vergil's description with the impression that we gain from studying the portrait of Henry. Vergil is probably more truthful because he wrote a few years after Henry's death, and was therefore not concerned about provoking the king's displeasure.

Francis Bacon's *History of the Reign of King Henry VII*, published in 1622, remained the major work on the reign until the twentieth century. He describes Henry as 'one of the best sort of wonders: a wonder for wise men', but 'for his pleasures, there is no news of them.' This implies that Henry was admired for his intellectual ability but that his lifestyle was rather colourless. Bacon intended his *History* to be more than a factual account of the past 100 years, and wanted his contemporaries and future generations to learn from it. Therefore he passed judgement on those who came under his scrutiny.

The greedy monarch in the famous nursery rhyme, sitting permanently in his counting house counting out his money, was based on Henry VII. Because he devoted so much of his time to replenishing the crown's empty coffers, historians have accused him of being a miser. In fact, his account books make fascinating reading, for we catch a glimpse of Henry the man, as well as Henry the king. From them we discover his weakness for dicing and playing cards, and the way he indulged his own and his younger daughter's love of music, spending 13s 4d on 'a lute for my lady Mary' and £2 'to the princess's string minstrels at Westminster'. This 'miserly' king was rash enough on occasions to pay £30 'for a little maiden that danceth' and £13 6s 8d on a leopard for the Tower menagerie.

A European visitor commented on Henry's sumptuous table, 'I had the opportunity of witnessing twice' for 600 guests. Henry spared no expense when entertaining those whom he thought would prove useful in circulating stories of his wealth. He was a

This painted bust shows Henry as he wished to be seen by his contemporaries, confident and healthy. The truth is that by the time it was made he was very ill having suffered a stroke.

keen sportsman, playing tennis and chess regularly, but his great passion was the hunt and he kept an impressive stable of horses. Henry is remembered as rather a cold man but the warmer, more human side was revealed on the death of his eldest son, Prince Arthur, when he rushed to comfort his wife, and when Elizabeth herself died 'he privily departed to a solitary place and would no man should resort unto him.' In order to gain a satisfactory picture of Henry's complex personality you have to read the available source material, which is limited, and then, having studied his policies, come to a fuller conclusion of your own.

2 | The Search for Security

Key question
How did Henry secure the throne?

Henry Tudor was King of England through blood and conquest. He was the male heir of the House of Lancaster through his mother whose own claims as heiress were ignored, partly because she was a woman, but mainly because in such turbulent times the warring factions needed someone capable of leading them into battle. However, it was the victory at Bosworth that secured Henry's claim to the throne.

Key date

Henry VII crowned king: 30 October 1485

Henry's first actions revealed his concern about the succession. Henry was keen to stress the legitimacy of his position, regardless of defeating Richard or his marriage to Elizabeth of York. For example, he dated the official beginning of his reign from the day before Bosworth, thus allowing Richard and his supporters to be declared traitors. This was doubly convenient because it meant that their estates became the property of the crown by act of attainder. Henry deliberately arranged his coronation for 30 October, before the first meeting of parliament on 7 November. So, although this body granted the riches of the crown to Henry and his heirs, it could never be said that it was parliament that made Henry VII king. This was significant because Henry could claim that he owed his crown to no man but to God alone.

Key term

Papal dispensation
The written permission of the Pope enabling a ruling monarch to marry or divorce.

Soon after Bosworth, Henry applied for a **papal dispensation** to marry Elizabeth of York. This was necessary because they were distant cousins. The necessary document did not arrive until 16 January 1486. Henry and Elizabeth were married two days later,

A gold medallion commemorating the marriage of King Henry VII and Elizabeth of York.

finally uniting the Houses of Lancaster and York. The inevitable delay in obtaining the dispensation conveniently ensured that no one could say that Henry owed his crown to his wife.

After Bosworth, Henry's most immediate and greatest problem was ensuring that he kept the crown. Although many potential candidates had been eliminated from the succession during the Wars of the Roses and their aftermath, it was not until 1506 that Henry could feel really secure on his throne. By that time the most dangerous claimants to the crown were either dead or safely behind bars.

Henry marries Elizabeth of York: 18 January 1486

Key date

Yorkist claimants to the throne

In 1485 there were still a number of important Yorkists alive with a strong claim to the throne.

- The most direct male representative of the family was Richard III's 10-year-old nephew, Edward, Earl of Warwick (the son of his brother George). Henry successfully removed him by sending him to the Tower. Although it was a royal stronghold, the Tower was also a royal residence, so Warwick lived in relative comfort, although without the freedom to come and go as he pleased.
- Richard III had named as his heir another nephew, John de la Pole, Earl of Lincoln (the son of his sister Elizabeth). Henry considered Lincoln, and his father, the Duke of Suffolk, as potential enemies. However, both professed their loyalty to Henry and the king accepted this. Lincoln was invited to join the **council**.

Council
Ruling council of the king, mainly composed of his most influential nobles and gentry.

Key term

Although Richard's supporters at Bosworth were naturally treated with suspicion, Henry was prepared to give them a second chance as long as they pledged their loyalty to him. The Earl of Surrey had fought on the Yorkist side with his father, the Duke of Norfolk, who had died at Bosworth, and Henry kept him in prison until 1489 when he became convinced of his good intentions. However, another of Richard's allies, the Duke of Northumberland, was released even sooner, at the end of 1485, and was given the opportunity to prove his loyalty by resuming his old position in control of the north of England.

Henry also attempted to ensure the obedience and support of two other leading Yorkist northern Lords. He demanded promises in writing that carried a fine, from Viscount Beaumont for his good behaviour, and kept the heir of the Earl of Westmorland at court. Ex-Yorkists were therefore not automatically excluded from the Tudor court: loyalty was the new king's only requirement for them to regain royal favour.

3 | Challenges to Henry's Rule: Pretenders and Protests

When Henry came to power he was a largely unknown and untried nobleman. He knew Wales, Brittany and France better than he knew England. Few of his subjects believed that the civil wars were over or that he would remain king for long. The uncertainty of his rule, the continuing political instability and the economic problems caused by war affected nobleman and commoner alike. Therefore, Henry had to deal with the disgruntled – protestors against such things as high taxes – alongside the dangerous – pretenders or rival claimants to the throne. Henry could not afford to ignore or treat lightly any protest or rebellion but it was clear that the main threat to his position came from the pretenders Lambert Simnel and Perkin Warbeck.

Minor risings 1485–6

In spite of his precautions, Henry faced minor risings before the first anniversary of his accession. Although, with hindsight, they appear rather insignificant, it was alarming for Henry at the time as he could not tell how much Yorkist sympathy they might arouse. Trouble broke out while the king was on royal progress to his northern capital of York. This was a public relations exercise in an unruly area, whereby the king showed himself to his people in an attempt to secure their support.

Trouble in the Midlands and the North

As Henry travelled north in April 1486, Francis, Lord Lovel, one of Richard's most loyal supporters, and the Stafford brothers, Thomas and Humphrey, also faithful adherents of Richard, broke the **sanctuary** they had been keeping in Colchester since Bosworth.

Lovel headed north and planned to waylay the king, while the Staffords travelled to Worcester to raise rebellion in the west. Henry heard of this while he was at Lincoln. Nevertheless, he continued with his progress, but sent an armed force to offer the rebels the choice of pardon and reconciliation or, if they fought and lost, excommunication and death. The rebels dispersed, but Lovel evaded capture once more and fled to Flanders. The Staffords sought sanctuary once again. The king and his judges felt that it was unreasonable for declared traitors to be allowed sanctuary a second time, so the Staffords were arrested and sent to the Tower. Humphrey was executed, but Thomas was pardoned and remained loyal thereafter.

Trouble in Wales

At about the same time there was trouble in Wales from a group of dissatisfied Yorkists drawn from among the Vaughans and Herberts. Led by Sir Thomas Vaughan of Tretower, they conspired to kill Henry and seize Brecon castle. The rebellion was put down by Henry's old ally Rhys ap Thomas, whom the king had knighted at Bosworth.

Here Henry's calculated mercy was apparent. His policy of severity towards the major ringleaders and clemency to the rank and file proved successful. The royal progress to the disaffected areas provoked the required reaction of loyalty and obedience, and Henry was seen as the upholder of justice and order. As if to

Key question
Who was responsible for the risings of 1485–6 and how were they suppressed?

Key term

Sanctuary
The Church offered protection from the law for up to 40 days but, by the fifteenth century, sanctuaries in major towns were sheltering people for indefinite periods of time, although this was a source of dispute with some kings.

Prince Arthur, from a stained-glass window in Great Malvern Priory.

put the seal on this success, the queen gave birth to a healthy son on 19 September at Winchester, England's ancient capital. The baby was christened Arthur, serving to remind people of the legendary King Arthur of old. The king was not yet 30 years old – young enough to have more children and to see his heir attain maturity.

Rebellions in Yorkshire (1489) and Cornwall (1497)

The rebellions in Yorkshire and Cornwall stemmed not from dynastic causes, but from reactions against the king's demands for money. However, they did influence the way in which Henry responded to the dynastic challenges and showed how delicate was the balance between public order and lawlessness.

Yorkshire

Henry planned to go to the aid of Brittany, which was being threatened by France, and the parliament of 1489 granted him a **subsidy** of £100,000 to pay for it. The tax caused widespread resentment because it was raised in a new way, as a sort of income tax. The king appears to have received only £27,000 of the total granted. The tax was particularly badly received in Yorkshire, which was suffering the after-effects of a bad harvest the previous summer. The people also resented the fact that the counties to the north of them were exempted from the tax because they were expected to defend the country from the Scots. Henry Percy, Earl of Northumberland, put their case to the king, but Henry refused to negotiate. When the Earl returned north with the news, he was murdered, presumably by malcontents.

The king has sometimes been thought to have been behind this murder as one of the 'murderers', John à Chambre, had been one of his ardent supporters ever since Bosworth. Nevertheless, the fact remains that when Chambre was captured he was executed.

However, Northumberland was not popular in the area because he had supported the tax, and a more likely culprit was the embittered Sir John Egremont, subsequent leader of the rebellion and an illegitimate member of the Percy family. The Earl of Surrey finally defeated the rebels outside York and Egremont escaped to Flanders. The king travelled north to issue a pardon to most of the prisoners as a gesture of conciliation, but he failed to collect any more of this tax.

He faced no more trouble in the north because the new Earl of Northumberland was only a minor and a ward of the crown. To ensure this Henry appointed the Earl of Surrey as his Lieutenant or chief representative in this area; Surrey had no vested interest in the north and his loyalty was guaranteed because the restoration of his own estates rested on his success here.

Cornwall

Cornish rebellion: 1497

It was another request for money that ignited a rebellion in Cornwall. In January 1497 parliament voted for a heavy tax to finance an expedition north to resist the expected invasion by the Scottish king, James IV, and the pretender Perkin Warbeck (see pages 36–40). The Cornish, who were traditionally independent, refused to contribute to the defence of the northern part of the kingdom to suppress an invasion which offered little threat to them.

Holinshed's *Chronicle*, first published in 1571, sets out the causes of the grievances of the rebels as follows:

> Flammock and Joseph [the local leaders] called on the common people to arm themselves and not be afraid to follow them in that quarrel, promising not to hurt anyone, but only to see them punish those responsible for the tax imposed on the people, without any reasonable cause.

In May the rebels set out from Bodmin and marched through the western counties, acquiring as their only leader of any significance the impoverished Lord Audley, at Wells. On 16 June, about 15,000 strong, they reached the outskirts of London and encamped on Blackheath. In the meantime, the king had diverted his forces south under Lord Daubeney.

Historians estimate that about 1000 rebels were killed in the battle and that the rest swiftly fled. Only Audley and the two original local leaders were executed. Despite the fact that the rising had been defeated, it was worrying that the rebels had been able to march as far as Kent before facing any opposition. Henry had been directing his attention towards Scotland and Warbeck and, as the Cornish rising was unconnected with any Yorkist conspiracy, he had not responded to it early on. The rebellion hardly endangered his throne, but it had shown that he could not afford a serious campaign against Scotland. Henry now attempted to come to terms with James.

Consequences of rebellion

The rebellions in Yorkshire and Cornwall were not in themselves important, but they complicated other problems. They affected the way in which Henry handled the pretenders since they showed that the people were not prepared to finance a major war in defence of the Tudor regime.

Figure 2.1: The geography of Henry's kingdom

Henry's diplomatic skills were tested to the full in the challenges he faced to his throne. He was fortunate in that rebellion was regionalised; many of his subjects were not inclined to take up arms, less because of their devotion to the Tudor dynasty than their apathy towards a conflict that had lasted far too long already. At times he had to negotiate carefully and, when there was no other choice, he had to resort to force. Henry himself seems to have chosen to fight only when absolutely necessary. This was slower but cheaper and, therefore, preferable for both the king and his subjects. As time went on the stability that Henry was working towards led many to be content with his style of government.

Key question
How serious a challenge to Henry's rule was Lambert Simnel's rebellion?

4 | Lambert Simnel 1486–7

Henry was king because he had defeated Richard III in battle. The nature of the usurpation meant that a rising from Richard's Yorkist followers, such as Lovel, the Staffords and Vaughans, was almost inevitable. However, if such a plot was to have more chance of success in the future then the conspirators needed a Yorkist replacement around whom they could weave their plans.

In the absence of an available Yorkist descendant, suitable candidates were found who could impersonate one of the Yorkist princes in the Tower. The careers of the two pretenders, Lambert Simnel and Perkin Warbeck, were of great significance to Henry VII. They presented a dangerous challenge to his hold on the crown – both because of their entanglement with other European states, particularly Burgundy, and because they lingered on for such a long time.

Origins of Simnel's rebellion

Oxford and its environs were traditionally Yorkist. So it is not surprising that the first of the pretenders originated from there. Throughout the winter of 1486 conflicting rumours circulated about the fate of the Earl of Warwick (see page 39). Many concluded that he must be dead, as he had not been seen for some time. In this unsettled climate, a 28-year-old priest from Oxford, Richard Symonds, seized his opportunity. He detected a striking resemblance between one of his pupils, the 10-year-old Lambert Simnel, the son of an organ maker, and the murdered sons of Edward IV. Symonds decided to pass Simnel off as the younger boy, Richard of York. However, in the light of fresh rumours about the Earl of Warwick, he seems to have changed his mind and to have decided that Simnel would now impersonate Warwick.

Symonds took his protégé to Ireland, a centre of Yorkist support ever since Richard, Duke of York (the father of Edward IV and Richard III), had been Lord Lieutenant or the king's chief representative there in the 1450s. The current Lord Lieutenant, the Earl of Kildare, and other Irish leaders, readily proclaimed Simnel as Edward VI. The pretender was also supported by Edward IV's sister, Margaret, Dowager Duchess of Burgundy, who

Margaret of Burgundy.
Why was Margaret
determined to oust
Henry VII?

was always ready to seize an opportunity to strike at Henry. She
sent money and a force of 2000 German soldiers to Ireland,
commanded by the capable Martin Schwarz. This formidable
support led the Irish to go as far as to crown Simnel as King
Edward VI in Dublin in May 1487, although they had to
improvise the crown, borrowing a coronet from a nearby statue of
the Virgin Mary.

Although the conspiracy began in the autumn of 1486, Henry
himself does not appear to have been aware of it until New Year
1487. In February 1487 a few lesser nobles were declared traitors
and Edward IV's queen, Elizabeth Woodville, and her son by her
former marriage, the Marquess of Dorset, were put under house
arrest and deprived of their lands. What exactly they were
thought to have done remains obscure.

The real Earl of Warwick was exhibited in London to expose
the imposter. But the problem was not so easily resolved. The

sudden flight of the Earl of Lincoln to join the elusive Lord Lovel in Flanders at the court of his aunt, Margaret of Burgundy, made clear the gravity of the situation. Lincoln then accompanied Lovel and Schwarz to Ireland in May 1487. It is probable that the earl had been involved from an early stage. Lincoln obviously knew that Simnel was an imposter, but possibly planned to put forward his own claim to the throne when he judged the time to be right.

The suppression of the rebellion

Henry showed his concern by offering a pardon to such long-standing rebels as Thomas Broughton. Broughton, who refused Henry's pardon, had been among Richard III's most loyal followers in the north-west. His continued opposition to the new regime, and his ability to evade capture, was a source of irritation for Henry VII. Henry was fearful, not knowing how many of his leading subjects would defect to the Yorkist cause when the crisis came to a head. On 4 June 1487 Lincoln and his army landed at Furness in Lancashire, marched across the Pennines and then turned south. He received less support than he expected because people were weary of civil strife. It was also the case that the reputed wild behaviour of the Irish soldiers dissuaded some from joining the rebels. The king, expecting an invasion via Ireland, was prepared and the two armies met just outside Newark at East Stoke on 16 June 1487. Lincoln's forces numbered about 8000 and Henry's possibly totalled 12,000, but many on Henry's side held back even on the battlefield itself.

The immediate attack of the experienced German soldiers and the daredevil tactics of the Irish severely strained the royal front line, but after three hours it was the Yorkist forces that were divided and surrounded. Lincoln, Schwarz, Broughton, and Thomas Geraldine, the Irish leader, all perished, along with nearly half their army. Lovel either fled or was killed: certainly he was never seen again. Lambert Simnel and Richard Symonds were both captured. Symonds was sentenced to life imprisonment in a bishop's prison out of respect for his clerical position. The king, recognising that Simnel had been merely a pawn in the hands of ambitious men, made him a turnspit in the royal kitchen. He was later promoted to be the king's falconer as a reward for his good service.

Henry's mercy was calculated. He could afford to be reasonably generous to Simnel because Symonds was now in prison and the real ringleaders were dead. As a deterrent to others in the future, those nobles who had fought at Stoke were dealt with swiftly in Henry's second parliament (November to December 1487). Twenty-eight of them were attainted and their lands were confiscated.

Some historians view Stoke as the last battle of the Wars of the Roses. Certainly, Henry never again faced an army composed of his own subjects on English soil, although further rebellions did follow. Indeed, Stoke could have been a second Bosworth, with Henry this time in the role of Richard III. What was most important was that Henry was victorious, in spite of the added problem of foreign intervention. However, the fact that such a

Key question
How was the rebellion suppressed?

Key date

The battle of Stoke: 1487

ridiculous scheme almost succeeded indicates that the country was still very unsettled and shows how fragile was Henry's grasp on the crown. It was no coincidence that on 25 November his wife, Elizabeth, and mother of his heir, was belatedly crowned queen. This was designed to unite the nation and to secure the goodwill of the people.

5 | Perkin Warbeck 1491–9

Further troubles arose for Henry in the autumn of 1491 when Perkin Warbeck, a 17-year-old from Tournai in France, arrived in Cork, Ireland, on the ship of his master, a Breton merchant. As he strolled around the town flaunting the silk wares of his master, his dignified bearing seems to have deeply impressed the townsfolk. They assumed that he must be the Earl of Warwick, as rumour was still rife about his whereabouts even though he had been presented in London. Warbeck denied this, claiming instead to be Richard, Duke of York, whose murder in the Tower was assumed but had never been proved.

The known figures behind Warbeck were men of humble origin. However, Professor Chrimes (Henry VII's biographer) believes that Warbeck's appearance in Ireland was 'no accident but was the first overt action in the unfolding of a definite plan'. He thinks that Charles VIII of France, and probably Margaret of

Key date

Elizabeth of York crowned Queen of England:
25 November 1486

It was hoped this would satisfy disaffected Yorkists.

Key question
How significant a danger to Henry VII were Perkin Warbeck and his supporters?

A sixteenth-century drawing of Perkin Warbeck.

Burgundy as well, wanted to use Warbeck to blackmail Henry if he became too anti-French over Brittany, which the French king wished to annex. The only direct evidence available is Warbeck's own confession, which he made on the scaffold:

> The French King sent an ambassador into Ireland ... to advise me to come into France. And I went to France and from there into Flanders, and from Flanders into Ireland, and from Ireland into Scotland, and so into England.

Support for Warbeck

The conspiracy achieved international recognition from the predictable troubled areas of Ireland, Scotland and France. Charles VIII welcomed Warbeck at the French court and by the summer of 1492 approximately 100 English Yorkists had joined him in Paris. The Treaty of Étaples with France (see pages 144–5) in November meant that Warbeck had to find a new refuge, so he fled to Flanders where he was accepted by Margaret of Burgundy as her nephew. In 1493 Henry showed how concerned he was by breaking off all trade with Flanders even though this jeopardised the cloth trade which was so important to the English economy.

In the interim, Warbeck found an even more influential patron than Margaret when Maximilian, the newly elected **Holy Roman Emperor**, recognised him as Richard IV in 1494. However, Maximilian did not have the resources available at that time to finance an invasion of England. Charles VIII gave Henry a respite when France invaded Italy in 1494 and turned Europe's attention southwards away from the problems of the Tudor dynasty; Henry could now concentrate solely on the revolt without fear of European invasion as well. His intelligence network of spies and paid informers had informed him who was implicated both at home and abroad, and in the parliament of 1495 a number of acts of attainder were passed.

The most important victim was Sir William Stanley, Henry's step-uncle and the man who had changed the course of the battle of Bosworth. Stanley had been overheard to say that if it could be proved that Warbeck was indeed who he claimed to be then he would not take up arms against him. As **Chamberlain of the King's Household**, he was one of Henry's most trusted officials and Henry must have been disappointed and frightened by his betrayal. His execution showed that Henry would spare no traitor, however eminent. Lord Fitzwalter, his steward, was also executed. It appears that a supposed adherent of the conspiracy, Sir Robert Clifford, revealed vital names to the king. It is probable that Clifford had been in Henry's service from the beginning, for he received a pardon and rewards for breaking the conspiracy.

The failure of the rebellion

The efficient work of Henry's agents and the king's swift reaction meant that Warbeck's attempted landing at Deal in Kent in July 1495 was a fiasco. He failed to gather sufficient local support and he set sail for Ireland, abandoning those of his men who had

Key terms

Holy Roman Emperor
Title given to ruler of territory now occupied by modern-day Germany.

Chamberlain of the King's Household
Official in charge of the king's household servants.

already gone ashore. He laid siege to the loyal town of Waterford for 11 days without success. He then departed for Scotland where he met with more encouragement, as the kings of Scotland always seized any opportunity to provoke their English counterparts.

Therefore, James IV gave Warbeck refuge and support. James IV hoped to stir opposition in England against Henry. It is difficult to be certain how far James was convinced by Warbeck, if at all, but he did go so far as to give him his cousin, Lady Catherine Gordon, in marriage together with an annual pension of £1200.

These actions were enough to challenge Henry's government and to threaten the marriage alliance with Spain, between Catherine of Aragon and Henry's son, Arthur, Prince of Wales. King Ferdinand and Queen Isabella would not contemplate sending their daughter to marry the heir to a contested crown.

James IV of Scotland.

Fortunately for Henry, the Scottish invasion of England was a disaster. Warbeck received no support south of the border and retreated, horrified at the manner in which the Scots raided and pillaged the countryside. James did not take advantage of the rebellion in Cornwall (see pages 31–2) to attack again. Disillusioned with Warbeck, he thought that Henry's conciliatory offer of his eldest daughter, Margaret, in marriage to James IV was more to Scotland's long-term advantage. In September 1497 a seven-year truce was agreed at Ayton which was formalised in 1502 – the first full peace treaty with Scotland since 1328.

Warbeck himself eased the situation by returning to Ireland in July 1497, hoping for more success there. However, as he found that even Kildare (see page 33) was temporarily loyal to Henry, he set sail for the south-west of England hoping as a last resort to find support from this traditionally rebellious area. Again he was to be bitterly disappointed; having landed in Devon, he was driven out of Exeter and Taunton and only a few thousand countryfolk joined him. Within a fortnight it was all over, and Warbeck once again abandoned his followers. This time he fled to the sanctuary of Beaulieu Abbey in Hampshire. In August 1497 he was persuaded to give himself up and to make a full confession of his imposture.

Since Warbeck was a foreigner, it would have been difficult under English law to charge him with treason. Henry allowed him to remain at court with his young bride, but Warbeck was not content with this and foolishly ran away in 1498. He was recaptured, publicly humiliated by being forced to sit in the stocks twice, and was then imprisoned in the Tower. As for his wife, she remained at court and became a lady-in-waiting to the queen. It is difficult to determine the truth of what happened next. Whether he was manipulated by the king or actually did enter into a ridiculous plot with the Earl of Warwick who was still in the Tower, we shall never know. His exploits had certainly tried Henry's patience to the limit. In 1499 he was charged with trying to escape yet again and this time he was hanged.

The Warbeck conspiracy

Key question
Who was responsible for the Warbeck conspiracy?

A week later, the Earl of Warwick was found guilty of treason and executed. It would indeed have been ironic if Warbeck himself had been used to get rid of Warwick. Although Warwick himself might not have been dangerous, he was always there for others to manipulate and weave plots around. Very probably, pressure from Spain encouraged Henry to act in this way. Ferdinand and Isabella wanted to ensure that their daughter was coming to a secure inheritance.

Warbeck maintained to the end that the plan to impersonate the Duke of York originated in Cork. However, there is evidence that he had learnt a great deal about the family of Edward IV from his former employer, Sir Edward Brampton, a converted Portuguese Jew, who had found favour at the Yorkist court. It has been argued that Warbeck's acceptance as pretender in Cork was part of a detailed plan and not a spontaneous reaction to public opinion. It is unlikely that he would have pursued his imposture

Key date

Warbeck and the Earl of Warwick executed by hanging: 1499

for eight years had there not been more important figures behind him from the start.

The most obvious person is Margaret of Burgundy, but there is no record of her meeting Warbeck before he left France in 1492. However, this does not mean that there had been no contact. Certainly, in the absence of any genuine Yorkist claimant at liberty, supporting Warbeck would have seemed her best opportunity to dislodge Henry. She would also have been a valuable teacher on Yorkist affairs. Warbeck himself appears to have enjoyed the imposture, revelling in the attention he received at a variety of courts in Europe. However, it is unlikely that he actually convinced anyone of importance that he was genuine, except perhaps briefly James IV whose ambition to humble the king of England in battle may have blinded him to the truth. Faithful Yorkists were prepared to back anyone in order to gain their revenge on Henry VII. Nevertheless, Warbeck did succeed in causing Henry eight years of considerable anxiety and expense that the king could well have done without.

6 | Further Yorkist Threats 1499–1506

Key question
How serious a threat to Henry VII were the later Yorkist challenges?

On the death of Warwick, the chief Yorkist claimant to the throne was Edmund de la Pole, Earl of Suffolk, brother of the rebellious Earl of Lincoln who had died at Stoke. On the surface, Suffolk appeared reconciled to Henry's rule, but there was underlying tension because the king refused to elevate him to the dukedom that his father had enjoyed. Quite suddenly in July 1499, Suffolk took flight to Guisnes, near Calais. Henry, fearing a further foreign-backed invasion by a rival claimant to his throne, persuaded him to return and he remained on amicable terms with the king until 1501. In that year he fled with his brother, Richard, to the court of Maximilian.

What remained of the old Yorkist support once more gathered in Flanders. Fate seemed to be against Henry: in 1500 his third son, Edmund, died; in April 1502 his eldest son and heir, Arthur, followed him to the grave. The king's only male heir was now the 10-year-old Prince Henry, then surprisingly (in the light of his later considerable athleticism) not very strong. The fact that Henry VII now acted more ruthlessly than ever before reveals how insecure he must have felt. Suffolk's relations who remained in England were imprisoned and, in the parliament that met in January 1504, 51 men, many of whom were connected to Suffolk, were attainted. This was the largest number condemned by any parliament during his reign.

The most famous victim was Sir James Tyrell, once Constable of the Tower, and latterly Governor of Guisnes where Suffolk had temporarily resided. Before his execution, Tyrell 'conveniently' confessed to murdering the two young princes, the sons of Edward IV, thus discouraging any further imposters. Henry seems to have been determined to pursue Suffolk to the end. This is not surprising if the report of an informer to the council about

Suffolk's flight is to be believed. It tells of secret meetings at Calais to discuss Henry's successor:

> Some of them spoke of my Lord of Buckingham, saying that he was a noble man and would be a royal ruler. Others there spoke of the traitor, Edmund de la Pole, but none of them spoke of my Lord Prince.

Henry's luck changed in 1506 when a storm caused Philip of Burgundy and his wife to take refuge off Weymouth. Exploiting the duke's weak position, Henry persuaded Philip to surrender Suffolk, whom he had seized from Maximilian. He agreed to do so on condition that the earl's life would be spared. Henry kept his promise; Suffolk remained in the Tower until his execution by Henry VIII in 1513. Meanwhile, his brother, Richard de la Pole, remained at large in Europe trying in vain to muster support for his claim to the English throne. However, few Yorkists now remained and Henry was proving a strong and just monarch to those who were loyal. Richard was killed at the battle of Pavia in 1525 but he had never proved a serious threat to the Tudor monarchy.

So Henry could not have felt secure even after the deaths of Warbeck and Warwick in 1499. It was not until 1506 that the persistent threat of Yorkist claimants was, for the most part, eliminated. Even then the security of the dynasty rested on the heartbeat of his only son, Prince Henry. Queen Elizabeth had died in February 1503, and Henry's fear for the future of his dynasty is seen in the way he searched the courts of Europe for a second wife for his remaining son and heir, Henry.

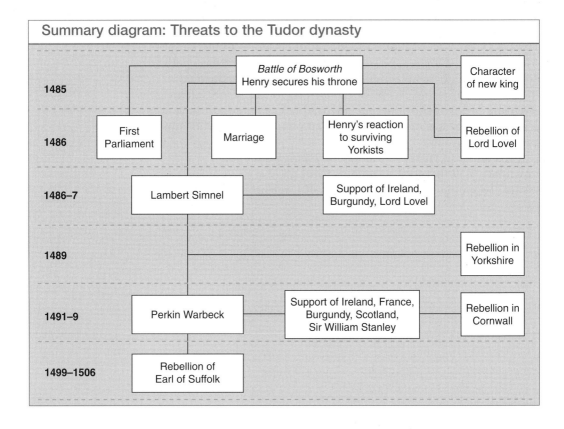

Summary diagram: Threats to the Tudor dynasty

1485			*Battle of Bosworth* Henry secures his throne	Character of new king
1486	First Parliament	Marriage	Henry's reaction to surviving Yorkists	Rebellion of Lord Lovel
1486–7		Lambert Simnel	Support of Ireland, Burgundy, Lord Lovel	
1489				Rebellion in Yorkshire
1491–9		Perkin Warbeck	Support of Ireland, France, Burgundy, Scotland, Sir William Stanley	Rebellion in Cornwall
1499–1506		Rebellion of Earl of Suffolk		

7 | The Key Debate

When did Henry feel secure on his throne?

Henry never felt entirely secure on his throne. Even after the capture of Edmund de la Pole in 1506, his brother, Richard, was still roaming Europe, although with little success. The king's only direct male heir was the young Prince Henry. He faced rebellions from his own subjects over demands for money, which showed that he could only rely on their loyalty to a limited extent. The challenge from former Yorkists, particularly the Earl of Suffolk, was unnerving, especially since they had sworn loyalty to Henry. Worse still was the threat from the pretenders, Simnel and Warbeck, because of their entanglement with foreign powers and the consequent fear of invasion.

It is easy to overlook how great these dangers were when reviewing the successful policies Henry pursued in other areas of government – finance, trade and the restoration of law and order. We must be careful not to forget the unstable background against which these successes were achieved. Henry learnt his lesson from Lincoln's betrayal in 1487 and implemented a more sophisticated system of well-paid and well-placed agents, which enabled him to detect Warbeck's conspiracy in the early stages.

The king was not vindictive towards his opponents and saw the advantage of using attainders against them rather than the hangman's rope. His two most notable victims were Sir William Stanley and the Earl of Warwick. Stanley's only crime was in agreeing not to oppose Warbeck if he were really the son of Edward IV. He was executed because of his closeness to the king, where treachery of any type could not be tolerated, and his death acted as a deliberate warning to others. Warwick probably died innocent of any crime except being born of Yorkist blood. After enduring the exploits of Simnel and Warbeck, Henry must have felt that Stanley was too dangerous a temptation to others for him to be allowed to live.

It is a credit to Henry's clear, decisive judgement and diplomatic skill that he managed to hand on his throne intact to his son, when the previous three kings of England had failed to do so.

Study Guide: AS Questions

In the style of AQA

'The pretenders Lambert Simnel and Perkin Warbeck represented major threats to Henry VII's throne.' How accurate is this statement with reference to the years 1485–99?

Source: AQA, 2003

Study tips

The cross-references are intended to take you straight to the material that will help you to answer the questions.

In this question you are expected to adopt an analytical approach in which the key phrase 'major threats' should be your main focus. In this way you will be less likely to offer a descriptive narrative. You must also evaluate the accuracy of the statement, for example:

- Did they or didn't they represent major threats to Henry VII?
- How strong was Henry VII's position?

It is important to remember that marks will be awarded both for the factual content of your answer and for the analytical skills you display, but it is not what you know but the way you use the information that is crucial. Indeed, it is important to remember that 'knowledge' counts for less than analysis in this unit because of the circumstances in which the essay is prepared. To achieve an acceptable mark there must be a clear focus on the question throughout. Your ability to successfully combine/integrate the two effectively will earn the highest marks.

You will be expected to place both Simnel and Warbeck in the context of the period 1485–99 (pages 24–42). (Note the dates. Do not be tempted to go beyond 1499.) There must also be an examination of why Henry VII's throne was so insecure at this time. The focus should remain firmly on Simnel and Warbeck and on those who gave them aid, for example, Margaret of Burgundy, the Earl of Lincoln and such foreign rulers as James IV of Scotland and the Emperor Maximilian (page 37). This might lead to a discussion of the way in which Henry's foreign relations were affected (pages 141–51).

However, in order to evaluate the nature and seriousness of the threats posed by the pretenders you must offer some contrast by briefly examining other rebellions, e.g. Lovell and the Staffords, William Stanley (see pages 29–30) and/or the strengths and weaknesses of Henry VII's position as king.

In the style of Edexcel

Study Sources 1–5 below and answer questions (a)–(e) that follow on page 46.

Source 1

From: Polydore Vergil, History of England, *written in 1513 but writing about the year 1495.*

When Robert Clifford came to the King, he was thoroughly questioned. He spoke about the members of the conspiracy and especially pointed out William Stanley. When he learnt this, the King at first grievously mourned that William was in the plot since he was Chamberlain and Henry had entrusted him with all his business …

According to Robert, William said to him that if the man Perkin was, whom he claimed to be, Edward's son, then he would never take up arms against him. Such feelings would indicate lukewarmedness towards King Henry, rather than treason. Yet, he openly admitted his offence, hoping that by a ready confession he would obtain his life from the King. Indeed, the King might have granted this, partly through mercy and partly to avoid upsetting Thomas, Earl of Derby, William's brother. But Henry feared such leniency to be dangerous to himself; … others would be encouraged by William's avoidance of punishment and would undertake a similar act of folly. William was condemned and a few days later beheaded.

Source 2

From: a letter to King Henry VII sent by an informer in 1503.

Sir Richard, the governor of Calais said that four years ago when the King lay sick, he [Sir Richard] was in the company of many important men. They were talking of what would happen if the King were to die and who would rule England. Some, he said spoke of my Lord of Buckingham and said he would be a royal ruler and gave him great praise. Others of them spoke of the traitor Edmund de la Pole. But none spoke of the Prince of Wales.

Source 3

From a print showing the hanging of Cornish rebels at Canterbury in 1497.

Source 4

From: Holinshed's Chronicle, written in 1571.

These unruly people, the Cornishmen, inhabiting in a barren country, complained that they should be so grievously taxed and burdened by the King's Council. Flammock and Joseph [the local leaders] encouraged the common people to follow them in their quarrel with the King, promising not to hurt any creature but only to see an end to the taxes laid on the people without any reasonable cause except for a little trouble with the Scots.

Source 5

From: Caroline Rogers, Henry VII, 1991.

So Henry never felt entirely secure on his throne. Even after the capture of Edmund de la Pole in 1506, his brother, Richard, was still roaming Europe, although with little success. The King's only direct male heir [after 1502] was the young Prince Henry. He faced rebellions from his own subjects over demands for money, which showed that he could only rely on their loyalty to a limited extent. The challenge from the former Yorkists, particularly the Earl of Suffolk was unnerving especially after they had sworn loyalty to the new regime. Worse still was the threat from the pretenders, Simnel and Warbeck, because of their entanglement with foreign powers and the consequent fear of invasion.

(a) Study Source 1
   What can you learn from Source 1 about Henry VII's decision
   to execute Sir William Stanley?   (6 marks)
(b) Use your own knowledge
   Use your own knowledge to explain the importance of
   Margaret of Burgundy.   (10 marks)
(c) Study Sources 2 and 5
   How far does Source 2 support the statement in Source 5 that
   'Henry never felt entirely secure on his throne'?   (10 marks)
(d) Study Sources 3 and 4
   How useful are these two sources to an historian considering
   whether or not Henry VII was a ruthless ruler?   (10 marks)
(e) Study Sources 1 and 5 and use your own knowledge
   Do you agree with the view that the Yorkists remained a
   serious threat to Henry VII's throne throughout his reign?
   Explain your answer, using these two sources and your own
   knowledge.   (24 marks)

Source: Edexcel, 2001 (questions (c) and (e); questions (a) and (d) adapted)

Exam tips
The cross-references are intended to take you straight to the material that will help you to answer the questions.

1. The answer to question **(a)** is to be found entirely within Source 1.
    You have to show that you have understood the content of the
    source. You do not have to use your own knowledge. This is a
    question on inference, i.e. what does the evidence contained in
    the source imply about the reasons why Stanley was executed?
    Keep your answer to the point. For example:

    • Stanley was too close to the royal family to be either ignored
      or forgiven.
    • Stanley's execution would send out a powerful message to
      would-be rebels that even those close to the king would be
      punished with death if they dared oppose him.

2. In question **(b)** you must use your own knowledge to explain the
    reference to 'Margaret of Burgundy'. For example:

    • She was a sister of Edward IV and Richard III and thus an
      enemy of Henry VII (pages 33–4).
    • She supported the pretenders with money and troops.

3. In question **(c)** you have to understand what is being said in
    Sources 2 and 5. Evaluate the extent to which Source 2 supports
    the view of the historian in Source 5. You will need to take
    account of the phrase 'how far', i.e. how far does Source 2
    support Source 5 and how far does it not? What are its
    limitations? For example:

    • The reference to 'important men' discussing possible
      successors to a sick King Henry in Source 2 supports the
      views expressed in Source 5.

- The fact that none of those involved in the discussion 'spoke of the Prince of Wales' as a possible successor may also be used to support the views expressed in Source 5.

4. In question **(d)** you have to focus on the key word **useful** and suggest ways in which an historian might find Sources 3 and 4 useful in studying whether or not Henry was a ruthless ruler. Remember the 'How useful' formula by focusing on the captions and attributions and ask yourself who said it and why.
    For example:

    - Source 3 shows clearly the punishment being inflicted on rebels – mass hangings. This suggests cruelty or ruthlessness but this was done according to the law of the time.
    - Source 4 suggests that the Cornish rebels were 'unruly' and that they somehow deserved their fate.
    - On the other hand, Source 4 also suggests that the rebels never intended to harm anyone but only aimed at persuading the king to remove the unpopular tax imposed upon them. However, the source was written much later (74 years) so that it may not be accurate. Also we must ask why Holinshed wrote what he did and how accurate and reliable he is as a commentator of events that happened long before he was born.

5. Question **(e)** carries the greatest number of marks, so deserves the greatest amount of time devoted to it.

    - You have to recall your own knowledge in order to discuss whether or not the Yorkists remained a threat to Henry's throne throughout his reign.
    - You must assess the contribution the Yorkists made to threatening the security of the throne by reference to the sources, the contents of which are there to help you. (You must resist the temptation to copy the source content but specific quotation is permissible if it is used to support a point you are trying to make.)
    - You must also show how ineffective the Yorkists ultimately proved to be and how Henry's policies – in foreign affairs and in respect of the nobility – also contributed to securing the throne and to defeating the Yorkist threat (see pages 40–1).
    - Be sure to focus on the key words 'serious' and 'throughout' so as to come to a balanced conclusion. You should round off your answer by offering an opinion in respect of how far you agree or disagree with the question.

In the style of OCR

(a) To what extent was Henry VII threatened by Pretenders?

(45 marks)

(b) How successful was Henry VII in establishing the Tudor dynasty?

(45 marks)

Exam tips

The cross-references are intended to take you straight to the material that will help you to answer the questions.

1. In question **(a)** you should examine and evaluate the extent to which Henry was threatened by rival claimants to the throne.

    Your evaluation should be balanced. You should also be able to come to a substantiated conclusion where an overall judgement can be offered, for example:

    - The weakness of Henry's claim to the throne and the way in which he became king might encourage others to try what he did at Bosworth (page 12).
    - Due to the frequent changes of kingship few expected Henry VII to last long on the throne (pages 4–6).
    - The nature and extent of the support for the pretenders – from some of the nobility and from abroad – suggested they posed a very real threat to Henry (pages 33–40).
    - On the other hand, Henry was well prepared to meet the expected threats from rivals and disaffected Yorkists (pages 35, 37–9 and 41).
    - The Pretenders did not have the depth of support necessary to topple a regime – the majority of the nobility remained loyal and he could count on the support of Spain abroad (pages 35 and 37–9).

2. In question **(b)** you should examine and consider the extent of Henry's success in establishing (securing) the dynasty.

    Your evaluation should be balanced. You should also be able to come to a substantiated conclusion where an overall judgement can be offered. For example:

    - The reign had survived for 14 years, longer than any of his Yorkist predecessors (note: Edward IV's two reigns – pages 4–6).
    - Henry had two healthy sons so the future of the dynasty seemed assured (page 3).
    - Henry had successfully defeated a number of rebellions and attempts to de-throne him (pages 28–40).

    On the other hand

    - There were still Yorkists roaming free on the continent, e.g. Edmund and Richard de la Pole (pages 40–1).
    - His foreign relations remained fragile and needed constant repair (pages 141–52).
    - He had not won the whole-hearted trust of all his nobles, e.g. Stanley's rebellion 1495, the large number of attainders issued (page 37).

3 Safeguarding the Monarchy: Nobility and the Church

POINTS TO CONSIDER

Henry recognised the importance of keeping control of the nobility and befriending the Church. Both had the wealth and power to challenge the monarchy. In order to safeguard the monarchy Henry employed a number of strategies to combat the disaffected nobleman and the disgruntled priest. These are examined in three themes:

- Henry's attitude to and control of the nobility
- His policy on retaining
- His relationship with the Church

Key Dates
1487   First law passed against illegal retaining
1489   Release from the Tower and restoration of the lands and title of Thomas Howard, Earl of Surrey
1504   Second law passed against illegal retaining

1 | The Nobility

Key question
What was the nature of Henry's relationship with his nobility?

The maintenance of law and order was vital to the survival of a medieval king. Discontent, disorder and rebellion were ever-present threats. To help him maintain the peace and security of his kingdom, the king needed both to make use of, and to control, the richest and most powerful ruling class in England: the nobility. The source of their wealth and power, and that of the king, was ownership of land and the title to which it was attached. Although the nobility were comparatively few in number, between 55 and 65, the king relied on them to provide him with the means to govern and police the provinces.

The stability and security of the realm rested on the nature of the relationship between the king and his nobility and their ability to co-operate. According to the teachings of the Church, the nobility had a duty to serve their social superior, the king, who was held to be God's deputy on earth. By the same token, the king too was obliged to protect them, to reward them for their loyalty and service and, above all, to rule wisely and fairly.

This theory of obligation, known as the **Great Chain of Being**, was the natural order of society. However, this theory did not always work well in reality.

The 'problem' of the nobility

The Wars of the Roses had temporarily upset this natural order of society with the crown being fought over by rival factions. This lowered the status of the monarchy. It was nobles who had profited most from this, seizing the opportunity to take the law into their own hands and acting as **quasi-kings** in their own localities. Although they had always tried to have the last word in their own area, they now took this a step further, using their servants and retainers as private armies to settle their petty quarrels and to make or unmake kings on the battlefields of the recent civil wars.

In 1485 it was this class over whom Henry had to assert his authority if he was to restore the dignity and authority of the monarchy. His problem, according to one modern historian, S.T. Bindoff, was 'how to suppress the **magnates**' abuse of their power while preserving the power itself'. A great nobleman had the power to provoke disorder and even revolt, but he could also quell rebellion and act as a mediator between the people and central government. Henry hoped that by imposing his will with ruthless impartiality, the nobles might learn to accept that their position was one of obedience, loyalty and service to the crown. If this was achieved, the rest of his subjects would follow suit, because the nobility were the natural leaders of society.

In this context it can be argued that Henry's reign marks the end of an independent feudal nobility and the beginning of a **service nobility**. Therefore, the purpose of this chapter is, in part, to investigate the role played by Henry in the transformation of the nature and function of the nobility, but also to examine the means he had at his disposal for imposing his will, the methods he employed, and the degree of success he achieved.

Size of the nobility

It is a common misconception that most nobles were killed during the Wars of the Roses, and that Henry therefore only had a small upper class to bring under control. This has been disproved by recent research, which has shown that the direct male lines of peerage families failed no faster in the mid-fifteenth century than at any other time in the later middle ages. In fact, there was always a high extinction rate, either due to death in battle or because peers failed to leave sons to succeed them. On average, in the later middle ages in every 25-year period, a quarter of noble lines died out and were replaced by new families through the creation of new titles. What Henry did to make his task of bringing the nobility to heel easier was to keep the peerage small by limiting the number of new lords that he created. This was unusual and in direct contrast to the policies of Edward IV (1461–83) and Henry VIII (1509–47) in whose reigns the nobility grew significantly in size.

Key terms

Great Chain of Being
The belief that everyone was born to a specific place in the strict hierarchy of society and had a duty to remain there.

Quasi-kings
Nobles behaving as kings in their own lordships with the power to make laws, impose and collect taxes and erect castles.

Magnates
The higher or more powerful nobility usually with the rank of marquis and duke.

Service nobility
Nobles created by the king to serve the crown.

Key question
How large and influential was the nobility?

Henry VII deliberately refrained from making new creations for three reasons:

- A limited noble class was easier to control.
- He so rarely elevated anyone to the upper levels of society that it was regarded as a particularly prized honour and distinction when it did happen.
- From Henry's point of view, most importantly, the grant of a title might involve the king in expenditure on quite a large scale. A title often brought with it large estates and, as these were usually granted from crown lands, the creation of new peers resulted in a loss of income for the king. If titles were handed out on a large scale, it could mean quite a considerable drop in the rents that the crown received.

Whereas Edward IV created nine new Earls, Henry created only three:

- His step-father, Lord Stanley, who became Earl of Derby.
- Philibert de Chandee who, in recognition of his military skill as captain of his mercenary troops at Bosworth, became Earl of Bath.
- Sir Edward Courtenay, who was vested with the title left extinct by the death of his cousin John at the battle of Tewkesbury in 1471, as Earl of Devon.

Even after Bosworth, Sir William Stanley and Sir Rhys ap Thomas, to whom Henry owed so much for his victory, were not made peers. However his uncle, Jasper Tudor, who had acted as his guardian and mentor through childhood and exile, was elevated from Earl of Pembroke (restored to him in 1485) to Duke of Bedford. Other than that, he created only one marquess (which he quickly rescinded), one viscount and eight barons during the remainder of his reign, as compared with Edward's two viscounts and 13 barons. Of Henry's creations only three were genuinely new peerages, which needed to be accompanied by grants of land.

The peerage consequently shrank from around 62 in 1485 to about 42 in 1509 as new creations failed to keep pace with the number of noble families that died out through natural, and in some cases, unnatural extinction (see Figure 3.1, page 52). According to one historian, T.B. Pugh, 'Royal intervention was far more effective than the failure of male heirs in diminishing the group of great magnate families'. He cites the case of Sir Walter Herbert whose claim to his late elder brother's Earldom of Huntington was ignored by Henry who thereby allowed the title to lapse. The fact that Walter was well known to the king, having been brought up with him at Raglan when the young Henry was put in the care of Herbert's father, the Yorkist Earl of Pembroke, counted for little.

Key term

Order of the Garter An honour was bestowed on the most important knights who became the most senior rank of knighthood.

The Order of the Garter
Henry found a useful alternative to the bestowal of a peerage on his loyal subjects, namely the award of **Order of the Garter**. This

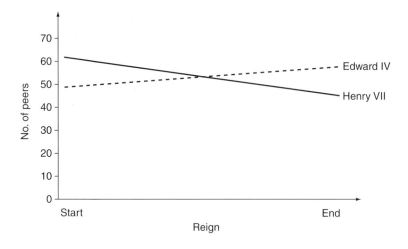

	Number of peers		Number of major peers*	
	Start of reign	End of reign	Start of reign	End of reign
Edward IV	49	58	7	12
Henry VII	62	45	16	10

*Dukes, marquises and earls

Figure 3.1: Number of peers between 1487 and 1509

was an ancient honour that involved it in no financial obligations; 37 of Henry's closest followers (including peers) received this privilege during his reign. Among those honoured were Sir William Stanley (later executed) and Sir Rhys ap Thomas but, whereas the latter embraced the award with enthusiasm, Stanley considered it scant reward for his good service.

Over-mighty subjects

Henry was fortunate in that he faced fewer of the over-mighty nobles who had so troubled Edward IV (see page 6). One reason for this was his lack of close male relatives; whereas Edward had had to cope with two powerful brothers, the Dukes of Clarence and Gloucester, Henry, apart from his step-brothers who were never made dukes, had none. The other was the king's cautious policy in rewarding his followers. The lands that came to the crown from extinct peerage families were not given away again. They were mostly retained by the crown, particularly the great estates that were acquired from the extinct Yorkist families of Warwick, Clarence and Gloucester.

Henry also controlled the marriages of his nobles, carefully ensuring that leading magnates did not link themselves to great heiresses in order to create new and dangerous power blocks.

Key question
What problem did the over-mighty subjects pose to Henry VII?

He was able to do this because, as their feudal lord, his permission was necessary for their marriages to take place. For example, when Katherine Woodville married her third husband, Sir Richard Wingfield, without royal licence, a punitive fine of £2000 – equivalent to the annual income of several hundred ordinary people – was imposed. That she was the Queen's aunt and had once been the wife of Henry's uncle, Jasper Tudor, Duke of Bedford, was never allowed to come between the king and his duty.

Some of these over-mighty subjects, such as the Percy Earls of Northumberland and the Stafford Dukes of Buckingham, did, of course, remain from the past. But such families were kept under close surveillance. For example, although the Duke of Buckingham came into his inheritance at the age of seven in 1485, Henry did not allow him to take possession of his property until 1498. Meanwhile the king acted as his guardian and retained the profits of his estates until the duke not only was of age but also had proved his loyalty to the Tudor dynasty. The Earl of Northumberland, who was murdered in 1489 during the Yorkshire rebellion, left his 10-year-old son as heir but he was not allowed to come of age officially until 1499 – again, not until the king was convinced of his loyalty.

Even closely related families with the potential to become over-mighty, like the Stanley Earls of Derby to whom Henry owed much for his throne, were kept firmly in check. In 1506, fearful of the family's growing wealth and power, most of which he had given them, Henry fined Bishop Stanley, his step-brother, the huge sum of £245,680 for illegally retaining (see page 16). He made his young nephew, the second Earl Stanley, pay over £1800 of the fine as a way of bringing him to heel.

So, partly through good fortune and partly through a carefully thought out policy, the greater magnates posed less of a threat to Henry than they had in previous reigns.

The key debate

Did Henry deliberately try to limit the power of the nobility?

Many historians have contributed to the analysis of Henry's relationship with his nobility, which remains a lively area of discussion.

Traditional interpretations

Traditional interpretations of Henry's reign argued that he quickly recognised the potential danger of the nobility and deliberately set out to quell them. The way in which the king thrust the nobility from their traditional advisory role on the council, and replaced them with professional lawyers and administrators was cited as evidence of this. This is now seen to be exaggerated and to some extent inaccurate. In fact, the 'truth' of Henry's relationship with the nobility is very much more complex and is the subject of continuing historical debate.

Recent interpretations

More recently, historians have tended to emphasise the fact that although Henry was suspicious of the nobility, he was not pursuing a consciously anti-noble policy. Henry did not know the majority of them because he had been brought up in Wales and France. It has even been suggested by Professor Chrimes that because Henry 'did not know the élite as he had not been brought up with them at court' his suspicion of the nobility bordered on 'paranoia', but this is probably going too far. Two of his closest companions were the Earls of Oxford and Shrewsbury, neither of whom, unlike the Dukes of Bedford and Buckingham, Viscount Welles and the Earl of Derby, was related to him.

Moreover it has been suggested by the historian Christine Carpenter that 'contrary to received myth, Henry had a court with courtiers and lavish court spectacle'. Indeed, many of those who attended the king in his court were his nobility. These included lesser nobles such as Barons Daubeney and Willoughby de Broke and great magnates like the Earls of Shrewsbury and Essex. This suggests that Henry was frequently in their company, that he got to know them and that he came to rely on them, particularly when he wished to impress foreign visitors and ambassadors.

On the other hand, one of the main reasons why Henry kept some of the nobility close to him at court was so that he could keep an eye on them. So, according to one of his most notorious agents, Edmund Dudley, 'he was much set to have the persons in his danger at his pleasure'. It is clear also that the nobility involved themselves in the political dynamics of Henry's court. Court faction and political infighting, so much a feature of the reigns of Henry VI and Edward IV, took on a more significant and sinister role in Henry's last years. Two notable victims of court politics are thought to have been Thomas Grey, second Marquess of Dorset, suspicion of whom had been 'stirred in Henry' by others, and George Neville, Baron Abergavenny, who was the only nobleman to suffer the public disgrace of being tried, fined and imprisoned for illegal retaining (see page 58). It seems that, whereas Henry mistrusted many of his nobility, he did favour a few. This imbalance may have contributed to feuding at court.

Like his predecessors, Henry recognised the nobles' importance to him in controlling the provinces in the absence of a standing army and of an adequate police force. He never attempted to interfere with their authority in the localities where they continued to dominate local government. Moreover, Henry continued the medieval practice of granting the overlordship of the outlying, and therefore more disturbed, areas of his kingdom to the greater magnates as a gesture of goodwill. So, despite his dubious support at Bosworth, Henry Percy, the Earl of Northumberland, was released from captivity after only a few weeks and was regranted the wardenship of the north of England. On his death in 1489 the king made his own three-year-old son, Prince Arthur, warden but with another magnate, the Earl of Surrey, exercising real control as lieutenant.

Yet, it has been argued that Henry's lack of instinctive trust in his 'natural partners', the nobility, may well have led to the undermining of local government. The problem, according to Carpenter, seems to have been Henry's 'lack of judgement over how to delegate and to whom'. The result in some areas, such as the north-west and Midlands, was feuding among the king's servants and a general degeneration in law and order.

Henry's attitude towards patronage

Key question
What was Henry's attitude towards patronage?

Key term

Patronage
The award and distribution of royal favours.

One aspect of Henry's treatment of the nobility that was new was his attitude towards **patronage**. Unlike his predecessors, he did not try to buy the loyalty of the nobility through the use of patronage. He was as careful in this as he was over the distribution of titles. The criterion he used in selecting those to receive royal favour was staunch service to the crown over a substantial period. This meant that it was not necessarily the nobility who fell into this category. The beneficiaries of Henry's generosity were quite simply valuable servants of the Tudor government. Some were peers, such as Jasper Tudor, the Duke of Bedford; the Earl of Oxford in return for his military support; and George Talbot, Earl of Shrewsbury, a notable administrator. But many were not. Edmund Dudley, the Sussex lawyer, who rose to become one of Henry's most trusted advisers, was not made a peer, but he 'used his title of King's Councillor as proudly as any peerage'. Loyalty and ability were Henry's sole requirements in his most important servants; patronage had to be earned, it was not an automatic privilege of the upper class.

Key date

Release from the Tower and restoration of the lands and title of Thomas Howard, Earl of Surrey: 1489

Henry's attitude towards punishment

Key question
What was Henry's attitude towards punishing the nobility?

Henry frequently used acts of attainder in a 'cat and mouse' way to punish disobedient magnates. After a period of time he would often arrange for parliament to revoke them, but he would only gradually restore the confiscated lands as rewards for actions of particular loyalty and support. Lesser nobles were sometimes forced to pay large sums of money for such reversals because they did not have as much to offer the king in terms of service or influence in their particular localities.

The career of Thomas Howard, Earl of Surrey, illustrates clearly how Henry was prepared to forget past mistakes if their perpetrators subsequently performed loyally for him. The earl's father had enjoyed the title of Duke of Norfolk, an honour bestowed on him by Richard III, and he had died fighting for his king at Bosworth. After Henry's accession, the earl was imprisoned in the Tower and both he and his father were attainted. However, he was released in 1489 and put in charge of maintaining law and order in the north, probably because he had impressed the king by turning down the chance to escape from the Tower during the Simnel plot. The attainder was revoked and his title was restored, but Henry only returned some of his lands – those of his wife and earlier ancestors.

After his success in suppressing the Yorkshire rebellion (see pages 30–1) Surrey was given back the core of the Howard estates but, in spite of his continued loyalty to the crown, he never received back all of his father's lands. The ducal title was also denied him and Henry kept this final prize to ensure his loyalty to the end. It was not until 1513 that Henry VIII finally rewarded Surrey with the dukedom for his leading role in defeating the Scots at Flodden.

Financial threats imposed on the nobility

Key question
Why did Henry impose financial threats on the nobility?

Henry also used financial threats to strengthen royal authority and curb the power of the nobility, particularly where he was suspicious of an individual but could not prove treason. In such cases he manipulated the existing system of bonds and recognisances (see pages 105–6) for good behaviour to his advantage. These were written agreements in which a person who offended the king in a particular way either was forced to pay up front or, like present-day bail, promised to pay a certain sum of money as security for their future good behaviour. This technique, sometimes with conditions attached, such as the carrying out of a certain duty, was used with all the élite classes as a method of ensuring their loyalty. Henry used the system not only to act as a financial threat against potentially disloyal magnates but also to raise much needed revenue for the crown. The sums stipulated in these agreements ranged from £400 for a relatively insignificant person to £10,000 for a peer.

As with his policy over acts of attainder, the greater the magnate, the more likely Henry was to bring him under this type of financial pressure. Typical was the case of Lord Dacre who was forced to make a bond of £2000 for his loyalty in 1506, which Henry could cancel 'at his gracious pleasure'. When the Earl of Kent was deeply in debt to the king in 1507 he had to be 'seen daily once in the day within the king's house' to ensure that he had not bolted.

Neither were spiritual lords exempt from such treatment. The Bishop of Worcester had to promise to pay £2000 if his loyalty was ever in question, as well as agreeing not to leave the country. But the most important noble to suffer in this way was Edward IV's step-son, the Marquess of Dorset. The king had believed him to be implicated in the Simnel plot and, after further treachery in 1491, his friends signed bonds totalling £10,000 as a promise of his good behaviour. When Henry was planning the invasion of France in 1492 he even went so far as to take the Marquess' son as hostage in case he seized this opportunity to rebel again. Towards the end of his reign, Henry even requested recognisances from those taking up new appointments. These would not be forfeited if they performed their duties in an efficient, loyal and honest manner. For example, the Captain of Calais had to promise £40,000.

This policy of Henry's has been much commented upon, not so much because of its novelty but because of the extent to which he used it as a way of curbing the political power of the nobility. Use of such recognisances can be found throughout the fifteenth century but other kings employed them more haphazardly and infrequently. However, for Henry they were an integral part of his policy for controlling the nobility by threatening financial ruin to any family that dared to offend him.

This did not mean that Henry was consciously pursuing a policy that was anti-noble. He appreciated the significance of the magnates to the fabric of society, but he was determined that any individual who chose to abuse his position should be firmly restrained. All the lords bound in such a fashion were guilty of offences that deserved large fines, but Henry showed that he was prepared to waive part of this if they would accept conditions that left them partly at his mercy.

One of the reasons for accusing Henry of bleeding the nobility in later years is because during this period Empson and Dudley were in control of the Council Learned (pages 74–5), which was responsible for exacting such fines. It was possibly because of their non-noble origins that these two ministers were particularly unpopular among the nobility, but it was more probably because they carried out their duties with such energy and efficiency. This degree of loyal service was what Henry expected from all his subjects, rich and poor alike. The nobility suffered most during his reign because they posed the greatest threat to his authority and to the security of his dynasty.

2 | Retaining

Key question
What was livery and maintenance?

Key terms

Livery
The giving of a uniform or badge to a follower.

Maintenance
The protection of a follower's interests.

Indenture of retainder
Agreement or contract binding a servant to a master.

One of the most serious problems that late medieval kings had to contend with was that of illegal retaining (the employment of private armies), a common practice often referred to as **livery** and **maintenance**. This was a common practice whereby great lords recruited those of lesser status as their servants or followers to help advance their affairs (by force of arms if necessary) and to increase their prestige. They were given a uniform on which was emblazoned their master's crest or coat of arms showing whom they served.

Kings had permitted this practice to exist because it could help the magnate control his particular locality and provided a quick and efficient way of raising an army, both of which were important to the king. Apart from these obvious uses, it was felt to be only natural that a nobleman should have a retinue of men of respectable social status. However, the recent civil wars had shown that these retainers could also create lawlessness at both local and national levels, and could be used as an effective force against the king.

Retainers could also be used as armed forces to threaten those who opposed their master. Interferences of this kind occurred to settle not only the lord's disputes but also those of his servants. This was because the lords had obligations to their followers as in the **indenture of retainder** they undertook to be good lords to their men. However, it was originally meant to be based on principles of honour and mutual respect, with a lord accepting the responsibility of advancing and protecting the interests of his client, but not where they clashed with the law. Thus maintenance was now all too often abused, with nobles frequently going beyond the bounds of 'good lordship'.

Edward IV's legislation against retaining

Edward IV's parliament of 1468 had passed a statute or law prohibiting retaining except for domestic servants, estate officials and legal advisers. However, this law was largely ineffectual because it allowed the continuance of retaining for 'lawful service'. Therefore, during Edward's reign, nobles continued to maintain their retinues using the excuse that they were doing so within the existing framework of the law. Indeed as many as 64 new indentures of retainder for one nobleman still survive from the years 1469–82 alone. Historians now conclude that Edward intended this statute merely as a public relations exercise and passed it to soothe the fears of the House of Commons but with no intention of strictly adhering to it.

Key question
How had Edward IV dealt with retaining?

Henry VII's attitude towards retaining

Henry VII openly condemned retaining at the beginning of his reign and two laws were passed against it, in 1487 and 1504. Yet historians have differed in their opinions of the king's real attitude towards this practice. Originally they identified this as one of Henry's most astute and innovative policies. However, as more research was undertaken into the fifteenth century, it appeared that he was merely continuing what he understood to be the policy of his Yorkist predecessor – of restraining rather than attempting to eliminate retaining. Certainly, he still relied on the nobles' armies to protect the interests of the crown in times of emergency. In 1486 it was the Earl of Northumberland's force that rescued the king from ambush in Yorkshire, and the army that he led across the Channel to France in 1492 was raised from many of his lords' retinues. Further, the wording of Henry's statutes against retaining appeared to support the contention that he did not really intend to stop the practice completely. The acts of 1487 and 1504 did little more than repeat the statute of 1468.

However, the most up-to-date research now concludes that Henry's attitude towards retaining was actually quite different from Edward IV's. Historians who put forward this argument begin by referring to the first months of the reign when the king forced the members of both Houses of Parliament to swear that they would not retain illegally. In addition, although Henry's statute of 1487 seemed to echo Edward's, Henry paid far greater attention to the actual interpretation of the law. The loophole over 'lawful' retaining was partly closed by interpreting it strictly and, although lawful retaining was allowed to continue, it was often accompanied by a recognisance to ensure the retinue was not misused.

Henry took this further in the legislation of 1504. This act was harsher than his predecessor's because it omitted the ambiguous clause on 'lawful retaining', and laid down much stricter methods

Key question
What was Henry's attitude towards retaining and how did he deal with it?

First law passed against illegal retaining: 1487

Second law passed against illegal retaining: 1504

Key dates

of enforcement. It also introduced a novel system of licensing whereby men could employ retainers for the king's service alone. To do this a lord had to have a special licence endorsed with the **privy seal**, and the entire retinue had to be listed for royal approval. It was only valid during the king's lifetime.

Key question
How successful was Henry in curbing the practice of retaining?

Problems with retaining

Evidence of Henry's success in curbing retaining is seen in the reduction in the numbers of retainers that magnates kept. Those they had appear to have been limited to the legitimate categories of servants, officials and lawyers. Studies of individual nobles, such as the Duke of Buckingham or the Earl of Northumberland, show that they might have got round official policy by employing more estate officers than were necessary. Nor have any indentures so far been discovered for Henry's reign similar to those of the pre-1485 period, which suggests that the nobles must have been very aware of the king's policy on retaining.

   If nobles did retain without royal permission whilst Henry was on the throne, they were careful not to leave any evidence. Those magnates who did break the law and were found out were made examples of. In 1506 Lord Abergavenny was fined the statutory £5 per month per retainer, which amounted to the enormous sum of £70,550. Although Henry suspended this in favour of a recognisance, the culprit had learned his lesson and was an example to other would-be offenders. This was a particularly extreme case, complicated because Abergavenny had also been implicated in the Cornish rebellion. A more normal example was that of the Earl of Devon who had given a recognisance not to retain illegally in 1494 and then had to forfeit part of this for breaking his bond.

   The biggest difference in attitude between Edward IV and Henry over retaining is seen in their reaction to their friends. Whereas Edward turned a blind eye towards the misdemeanours of those close to him, Henry treated everyone alike. Among those **indicted** for illegal retaining in 1504 was the Duke of Buckingham, the Earls of Derby, Essex, Northumberland, Oxford and Shrewsbury, and even the king's mother, Lady Margaret, Countess of Richmond and Derby. One of the most celebrated victims of the king's displeasure over retaining was the Earl of Oxford, a friend and highly valued adviser. According to Francis Bacon, in his history of Henry VII's reign, written in 1622, the king complimented the earl for putting on such an impressive show in honour of his visit and promptly fined him £10,000.

   Retaining continued well into the reign of Elizabeth I, so Henry certainly did not eliminate the practice, but he controlled it to a far greater extent than his predecessors and prevented it from being a significant problem.

Key terms

Privy seal
King's personal seal, made from metal and pressed into wax. It was a substitute for his signature and was used to authenticate documents.

Indicted
Legal term used to describe those charged with a crime.

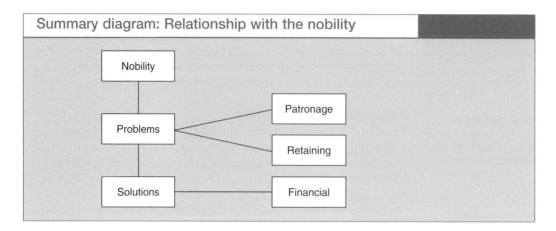

Summary diagram: Relationship with the nobility

3 | The Church

By far the largest landowner in the country, besides the king, was the Church. In 1485 this was the Roman Catholic Church and its first allegiance was not to the English crown but to the Pope in Rome. Although the Pope had no control over the day-to-day running of the Church in England, he had the spiritual authority to determine how the people worshipped and how Church **doctrine** was to be understood. The Pope also had the power to influence a kingdom's domestic and foreign politics by either offering or withholding his support for the ruler.

The Church was a powerful organisation that consisted of the **regular clergy** – some 10,000 strong – and **secular clergy** – numbering around 35,000. It formed a state within a state, with its own system of law courts and privileges available for the clergy, which rivalled the authority of the king. These courts dealt with religious crimes such as adultery and heresy and crimes committed by churchmen. Although this was potentially an explosive situation, crown and Church normally managed to exist side by side in relative harmony. Henry VII was a loyal member of the Church and did nothing to jeopardise this.

However, despite its size, power and wealth the Church did have problems. The chief abuses were poverty, **pluralism**, non-residence and ignorance. Many parish priests were poorly educated, some were illiterate, and their poverty contrasted with the wealth of the bishops. For example, 75 per cent of parish priests earned less than £15 per annum while two-thirds of bishops earned more than £500. In order to survive, many priests tried to serve more than one parish (in the worst cases as many as five), which affected the quality of religious worship. It has been calculated that of the 10,000 parishes in England and Wales a quarter were likely to be without a resident clergyman. There were instances of neglect and criminal activity by priests, which served to blacken the reputation of the Church. Nevertheless, in spite of its flaws the Church was generally popular with the people, whom it served reasonably well.

Key question
How stable and influential was the Church in this period?

Key terms

Doctrine
The rules, principles and teachings of the Church.

Regular clergy
Monks and nuns who devoted their lives to prayer and study in monasteries. They tended to keep themselves sheltered from the outside world.

Secular clergy
Parish priests, chaplains and bishops who lived in the outside world. They performed tasks such as marriage, baptism and burial.

Pluralism
The holding of more than one parish by a clergyman.

Key question
Did the Church hinder or help Henry VII in his government of the kingdom?

Key terms

Orthodox
Accepting without question the doctrine of the Church.

Excommunicate
To cast out of or exclude from the Church.

Henry and the Church

Henry was pious and entirely **orthodox** in his religious belief and attitudes. Although Henry was aware of the weaknesses within the Church he did not question its authority nor did he try to reform it. He was keen to maintain good relations with the Church because it could be a powerful ally in his claim to legitimacy and in his search for security. For example, in an effort to gain an international ally, Pope Innocent VIII was among the first foreign rulers to recognise Henry's claim to the throne. The Pope also supported Henry by **excommunicating** all those who rebelled against him. Henry responded by being the first English monarch to send an ambassador to Rome.

Henry's relationship with his bishops was equally good. He employed the most talented of them to serve him in government. The most senior churchmen – John Morton, Archbishop of Canterbury, Christopher Bainbridge, Archbishop of York, William

---

Profile: John Morton 1420–1500

c. 1420	– Born in Dorset, the son of a minor landowner
c. Early 1440s	– Educated at Balliol College, Oxford. Graduated with a doctorate in canon (Church) law
c. 1440s–50s	– Earned his living as a canon lawyer in Church courts
1461	– Joined the Lancastrians and was forced to flee abroad after the battle of Towton
1470	– Returned to England and made his peace with the Yorkist King, Edward IV
1473	– Appointed to government office as Master of the Rolls (responsible for government records)
1474	– Selected to go on an embassy to Hungary
1475	– Appointed to negotiate the Treaty of Pecquigny with France
1479	– Promoted and appointed Bishop of Ely
	– Became tutor to Edward IV's son, Prince Edward
1483	– Arrested and imprisoned by Richard III
1484	– Escaped to Flanders. Joined Henry Tudor and the Lancastrians in exile
1485	– Appointed to Henry VII's ruling Council
1486	– Promoted to Archbishop of Canterbury
1487	– Appointed Lord Chancellor and took charge of Henry VII's government
1493	– Promoted to Cardinal by Pope Alexander VI of Rome

Morton was especially trusted by Henry VII and, as a result, was able to exert a great deal of influence over the king and government policy. He was an experienced administrator and possessed the leadership qualities Henry VII needed to run his government. Morton's control and management of the Church ensured that it and its senior clerics remained loyal to the king.

Warham, Bishop of London, and Richard Fox, Bishop of
Winchester – became the king's closest and most loyal advisers.
Through their support for him, Henry was able to control and
exploit the power and influence of the Church. The Church
provided the king's coffers with substantial amounts of money
raised through clerical taxation, loans and fines. The bishops also
ensured that the parish clergy reminded the people of the
importance of obedience to authority and the penalties for
sinfulness and disorder.

Popular religion and the challenge of heresy

The parish church was the focal point of village life and its priest
the most respected member of the community. The majority of
Englishmen and women were devout followers of the traditional
practices and beliefs of the Church. They attended regularly and,
as part of their routine of life, they followed the Church calendar,
which marked the religious feasts, festivals and holy days. While
the priest's main preoccupation was the teaching and preaching
on matters of death and judgement, heaven and hell, the
parishioner was more concerned with baptism, marriage and
burial. The religious fervour of the **laity** was frequently expressed
in a materialistic way, and in the fifteenth century many of
England's 9000 parish churches were either built or improved by
individuals hoping that their generosity would help reserve a
place for them in heaven.

The only **heretical** idea to have acquired a significant following
in England in the later middle ages was **Lollardy**. This laid stress
on the reading of the Bible and urged the clergy to confine
themselves to their **pastoral duties**. However, systematic
persecution in the early fifteenth century had forced it
underground, and there was no resurgence under Henry VII.
About 73 people are known to have been put on trial for heresy
and, of these, only three were actually burnt at the stake; the
remainder confessed their sins and repented.

The Church as an instrument of control

Rulers were seen as God's deputies on earth acting as guardians
of His people. Therefore, any threat to the ruler or to the
internal peace and security of the nation was interpreted as a
challenge to God. On the other hand, when a ruler like
Richard III lost his life in battle it was thought to be an
indication of God's displeasure with His deputy whose authority
had rightly been challenged. Rebellion or any type of civil
unrest was abhorrent to most people from nobleman to peasant
because, as Sir Thomas Elyot wrote, 'Where there is a lack of
order there must needs be perpetual conflict'. This meant that
the worst fear for most people was an outbreak of general
anarchy.

The late middle ages were littered with examples of this type of
unrest: the Peasants' Revolt in 1381 against the **poll tax**, the Wars
of the Roses in the middle of the fifteenth century, and the
rebellion in Cornwall in 1497, again stemming mainly from the

Key question
How significant was
the challenge of
heresy to the
popularity of the
Church?

Key terms

Laity
The main body of
Church members
who do not belong
to the clergy.

Heretic
Christian who
denies the authority
of the Church and
rejects or accepts
only some of its
teachings.

Lollardy
A heretic movement
that supported the
translation of the
Bible into English
from Latin.

Pastoral duties
The duty of care
exercised by a priest
to his parishioners
such as baptism,
marriage and
burial.

Poll tax
Tax imposed on
individual people.

ill-feeling caused by what was regarded as an unjustified tax. On all these occasions, resentment built up slowly and people took up arms only as a last resort. There was little violence for the sake of violence.

The fate of Henry VI and Richard III acted as a warning to Henry VII of how an incompetent or unscrupulous monarch could be overthrown. Equally clearly, the Wars of the Roses showed him that, with the support of the Church, his subjects would quickly return to obedience if he and his bishops proved capable of asserting the right degree of authority. In the absence of a police force and standing army, Henry recognised the Church's important role in maintaining social stability and in ensuring people's loyalty.

The Church was able to exert so much authority over the people because of a concept known as the 'Great Chain of Being' (see page 50). It conveys the contemporary idea of God punishing those who rebel against their prince (treason) or who question the Church's teaching (heresy). It emphasised that those in authority held their power for the good of those below them, and subject to those above them. The concept is clearly expressed in Church doctrine and it was ordered to be taught as a normal part of the church service.

Humanism and the new learning

Key question
To what extent had the continental Renaissance and the printing press influenced English culture and society?

The dramatic cultural developments that were taking place on the continent in a movement that we call the Renaissance (the 'rebirth' of art, architecture and letters) came late to England. Mainly it took a literary form known as humanism, rather than the artistic form, which was more typical in Italy. Humanism was the return to the study of the original classical texts and to the teaching of the humanities as the basis of civilised life. It made its first appearance in England in the middle of the fifteenth century. Because literacy was confined to the upper levels of society, its followers were restricted to the educated class. The celebrated humanist scholar Erasmus visited England for the first time in 1499 and was impressed with the high standards of classical teaching being fostered by John Colet, Dean of St Paul's Cathedral and founder of St Paul's School. However, this was an isolated development and an extended humanist circle did not emerge until the reign of Henry VIII.

Perhaps the most significant event of this period was the arrival of the printing press, brought to England in 1476 by William Caxton from Germany. Edward IV was happy to act as patron and, from this point, a steady stream of major English texts and translations from French and Latin emerged from the press. This led to the growth of a wider reading public, the beginnings of the standardisation of the English language and the circulation of the radical ideas of Erasmus. Henry VII also made use of the printing press to spread **propaganda** justifying his succession to the throne and denouncing the rule of Richard III. Throughout this book you will find various extracts written by the king.

Key term

Propaganda
Method by which ideas are spread to support a particular point of view.

Henry patronised learning and encouraged artists, musicians, poets and men of letters. He established a royal library and commissioned Polydore Vergil to write a history of England. In the opinion of a modern historian Gordon Kipling, 'no previous English King had been so acutely aware of the political advantages of surrounding himself with literary servants'. It was the task of poets like John Skelton and historians like Vergil 'to present Tudor policy in as forceful and impressive a manner as possible'. Taking as his model the court of the Dukes of Burgundy, which was acknowledged to be the most magnificent in Europe, Henry wanted the English court to become the principal focus of cultural activity in the kingdom.

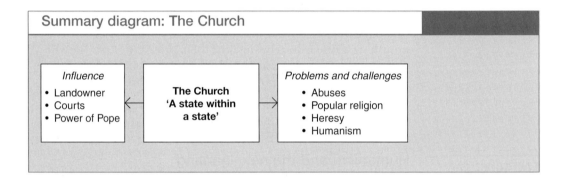

Summary diagram: The Church

Influence
- Landowner
- Courts
- Power of Pope

The Church
'A state within a state'

Problems and challenges
- Abuses
- Popular religion
- Heresy
- Humanism

Study Guide: AS Questions

In the style of AQA

Study the following source material and then answer the
questions that follow.

Source A

Adapted from: an Act for the Reversal of Attainders, 1504.

That the King's Highness from henceforth during his lifetime,
shall have full authority and power to reverse and repeal all the
Attainders of convicted persons and of their heirs that have been
convicted of high treason by Act of Parliament.

Source B

Adapted from: Francis Bacon, The History of the Reign of King
Henry the Seventh, *1622.*

The King was entertained by the Earl of Oxford [one of his chief
ministers] at his castle of Heningham. The King called the Earl of
Oxford to him and said 'My Lord, are these gentleman and
yeomen, which I see on both sides of me your servants?' The
Earl smiled and said, 'It may please your Grace that most of
them are my retainers'. The King was surprised and said, 'I thank
you for my entertainment but I cannot have my laws [against
retaining] broke in my sight. My attorney must speak with you'.
And for this offence the Earl of Oxford had to pay a fine of
15,000 marks [£10,000].

Source C

Adapted from: David Loades, Politics and the Nation 1450–1660,
1973.

Henry was bound to rely heavily on the aristocracy, both on his
Council and outside it. Henry liked to spread his trust and
favours more evenly, partly because he wished to conciliate
factions, and partly because he was aware of the jealousies
which would result from creating regional 'super-nobles',
however reliable and loyal. This he did by making use of the men
who were already great in their own counties.

(a) **Use Source A and your own knowledge.**
 Explain briefly the meaning of 'Attainders' in the context of
 government under Henry VII. (3 marks)
(b) **Use Source B and your own knowledge.**
 Explain how useful Source B is as evidence about Henry VII's
 policy towards the nobility. (7 marks)
(c) **Use Sources A, B and C and your own knowledge.**
 'Henry VII was successful as king in the years 1487 to 1509
 because, above all, he controlled the nobility firmly.' Explain
 why you agree or disagree with this opinion.
 (15 marks)

Source: AQA, 2003

Exam tips

The cross-references are intended to take you straight to the material that will help you to answer the questions.

1. In question **(a)** you should provide a developed explanation demonstrating understanding of attainders linked to the context, for example:

    - It refers to the crown's right to seize the title and possessions of an accused person by having them declared guilty of treason by Act of Parliament (page 169).
    - Henry VII used attainder or its threat as one of a number of means of controlling the nobility (pages 56–7).

2. In question **(b)** you have to understand what is being said in the source and who is saying it in order to evaluate its usefulness. You must consider its strengths and weaknesses, for example:

    - It was written long after Henry's death and may not, therefore, be accurate.
    - It was written by someone who was not that well placed to comment on Henry's policies (pages 160–1).

    Support your answer with some contrasting examples of Henry's policies towards the nobility, for example his use of the Star Chamber but his reward for faithful service, in order to explain what the source omits (page 72).

3. In question **(c)** you should evaluate the extent to which Henry's control of the nobility alone was responsible for his success as king, for example:

    - You must try to make effective use of the sources together with your own knowledge in order to provide a balanced answer.
    - You should provide a range of reasons in addition to control of the nobility, e.g. strong finances, concern with law and order, his use of such institutions as the Council Learned and employment of loyal and efficient officials (pages 74–5 and 99–100).

In the style of Edexcel

Study Sources 1–5 below and answer questions (a)–(e) that follow on page 68.

Source 1

From: Polydore Vergil, Anglica Historia, *written in 1513.*

The king wished to keep all Englishmen obedient through fear, and he considered that whenever they gave him offence they were motivated by their great wealth. All of his subjects, who were men of substance, when found guilty of whatever fault, he harshly fined in order by penalty which especially deprives of their fortunes not only the men themselves but even their descendants, to make the population less well able to undertake any upheaval and to discourage at the same time all offences.

Source 2

From: Francis Bacon, The Life of Henry VII, *published in 1622.*

He kept a strong hand on his nobility, and chose to advance clergymen and lawyers, who were more submissive to him. This policy made for his power and absoluteness, but not for his safety. I am persuaded this was one of the causes of the troubles of his reign. His nobles, though they were loyal and obedient, did not co-operate with him, but let every man go his own way.

Source 3

From: the recognisance made between King Henry VII and George Neville, Baron Burgavenny in 1507.

Indenture between the King and George, Lord Burgavenny: whereas George is indebted to the King in the sum of £100,000 or thereabouts for unlawful retaining, done in Kent, contrary to certain laws and statutes; and whereas the King may keep him in prison and take all his lands until the whole sum is paid, the King is graciously contented to accept as part payment of the debt the sum of £5000, payable over 10 years, for which payments George binds himself and his heirs.

Source 4

From: J.R. Lander, Government and Community, *published in 1980.*

The whole system sounds revolting. Indeed it was! But how else, perhaps, other than by fear, could Henry VII have controlled such a mob of aloof, self-interested magnates? After all, the entire justification for the presence of the nobility lay in its potential fidelity and its governing capacity. If its loyalty was not willingly given there could be no alternative to coercion.

Source 5

From: C. Carpenter, 'Henry VII and the English Polity', in B. Thompson (ed.), The Reign of Henry VII, *published in 1995.*

The nobility needed the King's power, and needed to make it work to protect their own land … on which their wealth and their power depended. They were unlikely to attack or undermine a system that made them what they were. The King had neither to force nor to buy their loyalty; he had it automatically by virtue of being King. Only a usurper, whose continued tenure of the throne was uncertain, needed to use threats.

(a) Study Source 1
Why, according to this source, did Henry VII punish wrongdoers so harshly? (6 marks)

(b) Use your own knowledge
Use your own knowledge to explain the significance of 'unlawful retaining'. (10 marks)

(c) Study Sources 1 and 5
How far does the argument presented in Source 1 challenge the conclusions of the author in Source 5? (10 marks)

(d) Study Sources 2 and 3
How useful are these two sources to an historian considering whether or not Henry VII ruthlessly suppressed the nobility? (10 marks)

(e) Study Sources 4 and 5 and use your own knowledge
Do you agree with the view expressed in Source 5 that 'The King had neither to force nor to buy their loyalty; he had it automatically by virtue of being King'? Explain your answer, using the sources and your own knowledge. (24 marks)

Exam tips

The cross-references are intended to take you straight to the material that will help you to answer the questions.

1. The answer to question **(a)** is to be found entirely within Source 1. You have to show that you have understood the content of the source. You do not have to use your own knowledge. Keep your answer to the point, for example:

   - To deter crime and rebellion.
   - To control the population.

2. In question **(b)** you must use your own knowledge to explain the significance of the phrase 'unlawful retaining', for example:

   - The recruitment and arming of servants by great lords threatened the power and authority of the king (page 172).
   - It also threatened the security of the dynasty and the stability of the kingdom (pages 57–9).

3. In question **(c)** you have to understand what is being said in Sources 1 and 5. Evaluate the extent to which Source 1 challenges the view of the historian in Source 5. Remember to consider 'how far', i.e. the extent to which the source challenges and, conversely, does not challenge the view expressed in Source 5, for example:

   - The reference to the nobility being motivated by their wealth and position into opposing the king in Source 1 contradicts the views expressed in Source 5.
   - The references to 'upheaval' and 'to discourage … offences' may also be used as examples of challenge or contradiction to the views expressed in Source 5.

4. In question **(d)** you have to focus on the key word 'useful' and suggest ways in which an historian might find Sources 2 and 3 useful in considering whether or not Henry VII ruthlessly suppressed the nobility. Remember to consider the origin of the sources and the motives of the authors in writing them. For example:

   - Source 2 suggests that Henry not only kept a strong hand on the nobility but also undermined their position of power.
   - Source 3 suggests that Henry imposed fines that were impossible to pay off.

   On the other hand:

   - You might argue that the deal Henry struck with Lord Bergavenny enabling him to pay off a much smaller sum suggests he was prepared to moderate his initially harsh approach to punishment.
   - You might also argue that Source 4 is more useful than Source 3 because it is contemporary, it is an official document and thus has no opinion.
   - However, Source 3 was written by an admirer of Henry VII more than a century after his death and so he is likely to be less critical and perhaps less accurate than Source 4.

5. Question **(e)** carries the greatest number of marks, so deserves the greatest amount of time devoted to it. You have to use your own knowledge in order to discuss the validity of the statement. You must interrogate the sources and assess the extent to which the fact of Henry's kingship alone helped secure the co-operation of the nobility by reference to the sources, the contents of which are there to help you. (You must resist the temptation to copy the source content but specific quotation is permissible if it is used to support a point you are trying to make.) You must also show how his other policies – in government, in finance and in the enforcement of law and order – also contributed to securing the compliance of the nobility (pages 52–9). You should round off your answer by offering an opinion in respect of how far you agree or disagree with the question.

In the style of OCR

(a) To what extent was Henry VII successful in restoring law and order? (45 marks)

(b) How convincing is the claim that Henry VII deliberately tried to limit the power of the nobility?

(45 marks)

Exam tips
The cross-references are intended to take you straight to the material
that will help you to answer the questions.

1. In question **(a)** you should evaluate and explain the extent to which Henry succeeded in restoring law and order. Your evaluation should be balanced. You should also be able to come to a substantiated conclusion where an overall judgement can be offered, for example:

   • Henry succeeded in demonstrating his power and authority as king by passing laws in parliament (e.g. against retaining) and enforcing laws in local courts (pages 83–5).
   • Henry outlawed the keeping of private noble armies, which had encouraged conflict and had contributed to the instability of the kingdom during the Wars of the Roses (pages 57–9).
   • The law was applied equally (or so government propaganda made known) to both noble and commoner alike (pages 86–7).
   • Contemporaries generally agreed that the kingdom was a more peaceful place in 1509 than it had been before Henry VII came to the throne.

   On the other hand:

   • He failed to prevent popular uprisings in Yorkshire and Cornwall (pages 30–3).
   • Some noblemen continued to break the law, e.g. the earl of Oxford was fined for retaining.

2. In question **(b)** you should test the validity of the claim and make an overall judgement:

   (i) By analysing Henry's attitude to and policy towards the nobility (pages 49–59).
   (ii) By examining whether the role, status and power of the nobility had changed during Henry's reign (pages 49–59).

   You must also focus on the key word *deliberately* which is open to interpretation and suggests that there has been some debate on the matter, for example:

   • Henry was suspicious of the nobility because they had the power to oust him from the throne.
   • He had to curb their power because they had been allowed to act too freely during the chaos of the Wars of the Roses (pages 4–6).
   • On the other hand, he relied on them to govern the localities, contribute to the pagentry of his court and support him in times of war (pages 49–51).
   • Although he punished some nobility he rewarded others for their loyalty (pages 53–9).
   • The nobility retained their wealth and they remained powerful but their role, status and influence became increasingly dependent on the will of the monarch (pages 49–59).

4

Establishing 'Good Governance': Government and Administration

POINTS TO CONSIDER
Sound and stable government is vital to a nation's
well-being. Henry VII was determined to re-establish law,
order and 'good governance' after the Wars of the Roses.
The way in which he did this is examined as four themes:

- Central government
- Regional government
- Local government
- Parliament

Key dates

1485	– Meeting of Henry's first parliament
1493	– Council in Wales and the Marches re-established
1494	– Sir Edward Poynings appointed Lord Deputy of Ireland
c. 1495	– Council Learned in the Law established
1504	– Sir Richard Empson appointed head of the Council Learned

1 | Central Government

The King's Council

Key question
What was the King's
Council and how did
it work?

The centre of medieval English government was the king himself
and the men he chose to sit on his council. The functions of the
council were to advise the king over matters of state, to
administer law and order, and to act in a judicial capacity in the
prosecution of nobles. During Henry's reign there was a total of
227 councillors, but there were not more than 150 at any one
time, most of whom rarely attended meetings. When all the
active members were present the council totalled about 40.

The difficulty in controlling the council led Henry to rely on a small, core group of councillors who met with the king regularly. This élite group included the chief officers of state:

- The Lord Chancellor, John Morton – responsible for administration
- The Lord Privy Seal, Richard Fox – responsible for the seals to enforce royal orders
- The Lord Treasurer, John, Lord Dynham – responsible for finance

and five others who held only minor offices or none at all: Sir Reginald Bray; Giles, Lord Daubeny; Sir Richard Guildford; Sir Thomas Lovell and Sir John Riseley.

The élite councillors who emerged later in Henry's reign included Sir Richard Empson, Sir Edward Belknap, Sir Edward Poynings and Edmund Dudley. These men gave stability to the new regime because Henry kept them in power for so long. For example, Morton served as Lord Chancellor for 14 years until his death in 1501, while Fox served as Lord Privy Seal for 22 years until the king's death in 1509.

In order to improve the efficiency of central government, Henry decided to use smaller committees formed from within the council, as his Yorkist predecessors had done, but on a more regular basis. Richard III had established one to deal with legal cases involving those who could not afford the high costs of the normal system. This latter committee was resurrected in the second half of Henry's reign as the Court of Requests, during which time it earned the nickname as the 'Court for Poor Men's Causes'. One of the first committees to be set up by Henry, in 1487, undertook responsibility for the implementation of the act of livery and maintenance (see page 57). Another was the Court of General Surveyors, which checked the revenues coming in from the crown lands and from those of which the king was feudal overlord.

The Star Chamber

Historians continue to argue over the existence of and role played by the Star Chamber during Henry VII's reign. It was mistakenly thought that in 1487 an act was passed which established a special 'Court of Star Chamber' to deal with the nobles; however, the only legislation passed in that year in this context was to set up a tribunal to prevent the intimidation of juries and to stop retaining. This tribunal seems to have gone out of use by 1509 and it had no connection with the later Court of Star Chamber. There were meetings in the 'Star Chamber' during Henry's reign, but this was a room in the Palace of Westminster with stars painted on the ceiling. Here the council met to consider judicial matters, but it was not a separate court in its own right.

Key terms

Gentry
Class of landowners
below the nobility
but above the
peasantry. They
were divided into
three social groups:
knights, esquires
and gentlemen.

Great Chamberlain
Chief official
responsible for the
running of the
king's household.

The personnel of government: clerics, nobles and the 'new men'

The membership of Henry's council differed very little from that of the Yorkists. The majority of its members came from the Church and the nobility and, of these, some 29 had sat on the Council of one or both of the Yorkist kings. However, it has been argued that the most important members of Henry's Council came not from the Church or from the nobility but from a third group, the **gentry**. Some historians have referred to this group as being 'middle class' because they were lower in degree than the nobility and higher than the masses. Others, such as Steven Gunn, have dubbed them the 'new men' serving a 'new monarchy'.

Clerics

The largest social grouping on the council was the clerics, who accounted for about half of the total membership between 1485 and 1509. Among the most favoured of them were John Morton, whom Henry VII appointed his Chancellor or chief minister in 1487 and Richard Fox, who became the King's Principal Secretary. Morton was a Doctor of Civil Law and he had practised in the Church courts, while Fox had a degree in theology and had studied in Paris. This sort of education and legal expertise proved ideal for administrators, which is why Henry appointed men like Morton and Fox to his Council.

Nobles

There was also a substantial number of nobles, which seems to weaken the case of those commentators who have claimed that Henry sought to oust them from government. However, what was different about Henry's council was that he demanded real service from those who sat on it, so that what counted was not noble blood but how loyal and useful a councillor proved to be. Those nobles who served him well were amply rewarded. Among these was John de Vere, the Earl of Oxford, who had supported Henry since his days in exile; he was given the offices of **Great Chamberlain** and Lord Admiral. Jasper Tudor received the dukedom of Bedford and the control of Wales.

Henry wisely did not wish to alienate the former Yorkists permanently, so, once they had paid in some way for their 'treachery', they were given opportunities to prove their loyalty to the new regime. The Earl of Lincoln was a member of the council until he joined the Simnel rebellion, while Thomas Howard, Earl of Surrey, became a councillor after his release from the Tower and was appointed Lord Treasurer of England in 1501. Although Henry's council contained numerous representatives of the nobility, only his uncle, the Duke of Bedford, his friend, the Earl of Oxford, and his step-father, Lord Stanley, the Earl of Derby, were really close to the king. It was probably this fact that gave rise to his reputation for being anti-noble.

'New men'

Henry did not rely on a particular nobleman or family as Edward IV and Richard III had done. Instead, Henry's chief advisers and servants were drawn from the ranks of the lesser landowners or gentry, and from the professional classes (especially lawyers) – men like Sir Reginald Bray, Edmund Dudley and Sir Edward Poynings. This has led some historians to label them the 'new men' because they were not noble and they did not come from families with a tradition of royal service.

Although Henry made less use of the nobility in central government than his predecessors, there was nothing particularly 'new' about his reliance on the gentry rather than on the aristocracy. For example, two of Richard III's most loyal servants – Sir William Catesby and Sir Richard Ratcliffe – were lawyers and came from landowning gentry families. The ancestors of these 'new men' had generations of experience in local government, justice and landowning. As Henry was exploiting his lands through more efficient methods of estate management, he needed servants who understood auditing and property laws and had administrative skills. Real ability in these areas was what mattered to Henry, not social class. The king himself was usually present at council meetings so he was very aware of how much individual councillors contributed.

The Council Learned in the Law

The most famous, some might say infamous, committee begun under Henry was the Council Learned in the Law. The Council Learned in the Law (normally referred to simply as the Council Learned) was a small and very professional body. Its name derived from the fact that most of its members had some sort of legal training or experience. This council came into being in 1495 to defend the king's position as a feudal landlord. Initially, it began as an offshoot of the Duchy of Lancaster (see page 00) and the Chancellor of the Duchy was in charge of it, but it grew rapidly to embrace dealings in all the crown's lands and the rights that accompanied them. It was responsible for keeping up to date with the wardship, marriage and payments on inheriting property of all the king's tenants, and the collection of the feudal dues that were owed to him.

Contemporaries criticised it because it operated without a jury, but this was true of all the conciliar committees. In fact, it was done deliberately because of the frequent charges of bribery brought against juries. The Council Learned was particularly hated because of its connection with bonds and recognisances (see pages 105–6) as it supervised the collection of these financial agreements. By the end of the reign it had become the most detested, but the most important of all Henry's institutions of government involved in the maintenance of law and order.

The Council Learned became increasingly feared after the promotion of Sir Richard Empson to the Chancellorship of the Duchy and the Presidency of the Council Learned in 1504. Under the joint leadership of Empson and his colleague

Key question
What was the Council Learned in the Law and how effective was it?

Key date
Council Learned in the Law established and entrusted with the task of defending the king's rights as a feudal landlord: c. 1495

This sixteenth-century painting suggests Henry VII conspired with his two most hated councillors.

Key date

Sir Richard Empson appointed head of the Council Learned. He ran it with ruthless efficiency imposing financial penalties on the nobility: 1504

Edmund Dudley, royal rights were scrupulously enforced. Henry's disciplinary use of financial penalties, such as bonds and recognisances, was certainly an effective way of keeping the peace, but under the management of these two councillors the practice seems to have become much more widespread. As Henry was, by this time, more secure than ever before, the harsh enforcement of such penalties by Empson and Dudley, through this council, was bitterly resented. They are also thought to have manipulated the system by falsely claiming that people owed feudal dues, such as wardship, where no such obligation existed. In fact, Dudley later confessed that he had acted illegally for the king in more than 80 cases. So hated had the pair become that on the Henry's death they were toppled in a palace *coup* led by the king's other servants. Within months of King Henry VIII's coronation Empson and Dudley were executed.

2 | Regional Government

The Provincial Councils are a good example of how Henry extended the authority of central government into the provinces. By relying on trusted servants like Jasper Tudor in Wales, the Earl of Surrey in the North and Sir Edward Poynings in Ireland to enforce his will in the outlying areas, Henry was ensuring that personal government was felt in every corner of his realm.

Key question
How was the North governed?

The Council of the North

The Council of the North originated in Yorkist times and was based in the city of York. Its primary function was to ensure the good governance of a lawless and undisciplined region that was too remote from London to be effectively controlled from there. In addition, it was given responsibility to oversee the defence of the northern counties of England, which were vulnerable to attack from a hostile Scotland. The Council continued to function throughout Henry VII's reign, supporting whosoever the king chose to send as his representative to govern there.

This region of the north was a frontier zone, and it soon became clear to Henry that he had no choice but to entrust the defence of the border to great border families likes the Percys. Henry reluctantly released Henry Percy, Earl of Northumberland, from the Tower and, despite the earl's Yorkist sympathies, appointed him as his lieutenant in the north in 1486. After the earl's death in 1489, Henry appointed another former Yorkist, Thomas Howard, Earl of Surrey, to succeed him. Surrey governed the north effectively and gradually earned the king's trust.

The Council of the North differed from the conciliar committees in having a clearly defined function dating from before Henry came to the throne. Yet it was closely linked to the main council, enjoying similar administrative and judicial power to enable the law to be enforced swiftly and efficiently, and, of course, it was ultimately subordinate to the king. Unlike his predecessors, Henry required his council in London to keep a close watch on the activities of his provincial council. In addition, Henry made sure that key members of the council were appointed by him rather than by his lieutenants. For example, one of the most important officials on Surrey's council, William Sever, Bishop of Carlisle, was appointed by the king to enforce his **prerogative rights** in the north. Sever was also required to keep in regular contact with Sir Reginald Bray in London with whom he worked closely to ensure the smooth running of the north.

Wales

Wales consisted of the Principality (made up of what later became the counties of Anglesey, Caernarfon, Merioneth, Cardigan and Carmarthen) and the Marcher lordships. Ruled since 1301 by the king's eldest son, the Principality was acknowledged to be separate from England, hence its shires did not return members to parliament.

The lordships of the March were relics of the piecemeal Norman/English conquest of Wales in the two centuries before 1282. These had their own systems of government, different from each other and from that of England. Both the Principality and the lordships owed allegiance to the king of England and he had ultimate control over them, but the absence of continuous effective rule from London had resulted in frequent outbreaks of disorder. This disorder was particularly marked during the Wars of the Roses, when it was famously said that, 'the King's writ [written orders] did not run' in the March.

With the freedom to raise troops for war, the Marcher lords were drawn into the dynastic conflict on the side of both Yorkists and Lancastrians. Until Edward IV established a Council to govern Wales in 1471, no attempt had been made to weld

Key term

Prerogative rights The rights and privileges held by the monarchy such as the right to tax, lead the nation in war and dispense justice.

Key question How was Wales governed at this time?

Key date

Council in Wales and the Marches re-established after an absence of some 12 years: 1493

together into a single system the counties and lordships of the Principality and March, or to abolish the privileges of the individual Marchers lords. Although Edward succeeded in neither respect, his Council had improved the situation in Wales by restraining 'the wild Welshmen and the evil disposed persons from their accustomed murders and outrages'. More importantly, his Council had set a good example, which Henry was determined to follow.

Key term

Marcher lordships
Territories conquered from the Welsh between 1066 and 1282 and held as personal property by the English lords who captured them. By the beginning of Henry VII's reign they numbered about 50 lordships located along the south coast of Wales and on either side of the modern boundary between England and Wales.

Like Edward IV, Henry appreciated the need for administrative order. This is why he appointed his uncle, Jasper Tudor, to govern Wales, and why later, around 1493, he revived the Council appointing his seven-year-old son Arthur as its nominal head as Prince of Wales. Although Henry's own experience pointed out to him the danger of an invasion of England through Wales (see pages 15–16), unlike Richard III, he did not have to worry too much about a possible threat to his position from the Welsh. His family links and Welsh connections, highlighted and celebrated by native poets and writers, ensured for him the support of the people. He rewarded their faith in him by trusting them to see to their own affairs, hence his policy of appointing Welshmen to key positions in Wales. For example, Sir Rhys ap Thomas was appointed to govern south-west Wales while William ap Gruffudd ruled in the north.

Henry's control of Wales was helped by the fact that, by 1495, due in part to inheritance and purchase, and on account of death and forfeiture, scarcely half a dozen **Marcher lordships** remained in private hands. Henry, therefore, governed directly, and indirectly, a larger proportion of Wales than any king had done before.

Ireland

Key question
How was Ireland governed at this time?

Key date

Sir Edward Poynings appointed Lord Deputy of Ireland: 1494

Henry arranged the passage of what became known as Poyning's Law. This decreed that Irish parliaments could be called and pass laws only with the prior approval of the king.

As king of England, Henry was also lord of Ireland. However, the island was not ruled in a conciliar way. The king appointed a Lord Lieutenant (in 1485 it was Jasper Tudor), but this was an honorary position. The actual work of governing Ireland was carried out by a Lord Deputy. Ireland presented a far more difficult problem to Henry than any of the other outlying areas of the kingdom. Only in the English Pale, a narrow band of territory about 50 miles long to the north and west of Dublin, was the king's authority really felt. In the rest of the island the effective rulers were the Anglo-Irish lords (descendants of English settlers who had come over earlier in the middle ages) and Irish chieftains, with family loyalties similar to the Scottish clans. Of these the Geraldine and Butler families were the most important. No English king had been able to dominate these lords and so Ireland remained very much a law into itself.

At the beginning of the reign, the Geraldine family held the most important offices, those of Lord Deputy and Chancellor of Ireland. Henry's predecessors had found that it was easier to bestow these positions on the Irish leaders if they wanted to avoid conflict. Henry quickly learnt the danger that Ireland could pose when Simnel and Warbeck received considerable support there. In 1492, after the Earl of Kildare (the leader of the Geraldine family) had recognised Perkin Warbeck's claim to the throne, the king deprived him of his position as Lord Deputy and his brother of the **Great Seal**. Only after they had sought the king's pardon in person was Henry willing to restore their titles.

Reorganising the Irish government

In 1494, Henry set about reorganising Irish government. He created his infant son, Prince Henry, Lord Lieutenant, so as to echo the nominal headship exercised by his elder son in Wales, and appointed Sir Edward Poynings, one of his most trusted advisers, as Deputy. Further appointments of Englishmen followed to emphasise Henry's desire for obedience to England. Poynings' main task was to bring Ulster, the most rebellious area, under the king's control and to impose a constitution on Ireland that would ensure its future obedience to the English crown. However, he failed in Ulster, only succeeding in buying the clans off in return for a temporary promise of peace.

He was more successful in the establishment of a **constitution** at the parliament that met at Drogheda in 1494; Poynings' Law, as it became known, decreed that an Irish parliament could only be summoned and pass laws with the king's prior approval. No future legislation was to be discussed unless it had first been agreed by the king and his council. In addition, any law made in England would automatically apply to Ireland. This gave the king far greater control over Ireland by destroying the independent legislative power of the Irish parliament.

In the short term, he hoped to prevent the calling of an unauthorised Irish parliament, which might recognise another pretender. In the long term, it proved to be largely a theoretical victory. The expense of attempting to rule Ireland directly soon proved to be unsustainably high, and the experiment was abandoned. Henry returned to his earlier policy of ruling through the Irish chieftains. He is reported to have responded to the comment that all England could not rule Kildare, that 'Kildare had therefore better rule all Ireland!' Kildare was reinstated as Lord Deputy and, for much of the rest of the reign, Ireland ceased to be a problem for Henry.

3 | Local Government

Local government was carried out in each of the 50 or so counties of England by a complex network of local officials who were directly responsible to the king. The king communicated with them through written orders known as writs, and their work was checked by judges and **commissioners** at regular intervals. The two most important royal officials in each county were the sheriff and the Justice of the Peace.

Key terms

Great Seal
Only documents and orders bearing the Great Seal were lawful and could be enforced.

Constitution
Set of rules by which a country or state is run.

Commissioners
Officials appointed by the crown to deal with specific tasks or duties.

Key question
How did Henry extend the power of the crown into the localities?

The sheriffs

The sheriff was appointed annually from among the local landowners in each county and was the closest thing Tudor England had to a police officer. He kept the king's peace and was responsible for the arrest, detention and prosecution of criminals. The sheriff was as much a judge as a law officer and he had his own court where he administered the king's laws. He also organised and supervised elections to parliament and MPs could only take their seats if they had the sheriff's writ to confirm their election. The sheriff also had a military role, being responsible for supervising the muster of the militia, local men who were drafted to serve a period in the service of the crown. Although sheriffs continued to play an important role in local justice and administration, they had gradually been replaced by the Justices of the Peace as the chief local government officers.

The Justices of the Peace (JPs)

The JPs were appointed annually from among the local landowners, the average number commissioned for a county being about 18. The local bishop would usually head the list of those appointed, with the lay landowners following in strict order of social precedence. Although some of the largest landowners were sometimes chosen to be JPs, it was the knights and esquires who carried out the majority of the JP's duties on a daily basis.

JPs were responsible for:

- The defence of public order.
- Implementing the various statutes of a social and economic nature, such as those concerned with the regulation of wages and the guilds.
- Dispensing justice to the criminals brought before them by the sheriffs. Four times a year they were required to meet in Quarter Sessions so that they could try those accused of the more serious crimes – except treason, which was left to the council to investigate.

Although JPs had the authority to pass judgement on all other crimes, more difficult cases were traditionally passed to the Assize Courts. The Assizes were sessions held twice a year in each county in England by professional judges acting under special commission from the crown. The position of JP did not carry with it any form of payment, as it had always been felt that to offer rewards for such work would be inappropriate as it was thought to be a natural part of the landowning classes' responsibility to ensure an effective system of law enforcement. As property owners, it was also in their own self-interest to do so.

Extending the powers of the JPs

After 1485 JPs continued to be selected from those with significant amounts of land. However, like Edward IV, Henry VII frequently chose to rely on the second rank of each county's landowners. This was another way of weakening the power of the greater magnates, which had led to the corruption of justice at the local level so often in the past. He also followed the example of his predecessor in widening the scope of JPs' responsibilities. In 1461 Edward IV had transferred the power to try criminal offences committed within the county from the sheriff to them. In 1485 an act of parliament gave them power to arrest and question poachers or hunters in disguise, because this could be a cover for murder or rebellion. Two years later they were given the power to grant bail to those awaiting trial.

Further acts in 1495 dealt with the problem of corrupt or intimidated juries, which had often been used by men of influence as a way of escaping punishment. JPs were given the power to replace suspect members of juries, to act in cases of non-capital offences without a jury, and also to reward their informers. Of course, Henry had to rely on the Justices' own self-interest as leaders of society for the upholding of law and order. Virtually his only control over them was the threat of removal from the commission if they acted improperly, which would be regarded by most JPs as a considerable social disgrace.

Limitations to the powers of JPs

However, JPs had only limited powers. Just as the king was dependent on them for the maintenance of law and order in the counties, so they were dependent on lesser officials in the countryside to bring offenders to them. By law every hundred (a subdivision of a county) had to provide itself with a High Constable and every parish with a Petty Constable. However, this was not easily done as people found such responsibility made them unpopular and there was no significant fee for doing the job. Frequently JPs had to apply considerable pressure to fill these positions and, as a result, many petty crimes went unpunished.

The Court of the King's Bench could override decisions made at a Quarter Session and, after 1485, JPs were commanded to read out a proclamation at the beginning of each session emphasising that grievances against Justices could be taken to either an Assize Judge or the king. But neither of these enactments seems to have been very effective. Therefore, although Henry had made provision for flaws in the system to be corrected, the new appeal system does not appear to have been widely used. The weakness in this type of local government was that the king was dependent on the goodwill of his officials; a system of paid servants, as existed in France, would have been more efficient. However, given the financial constraints on the English crown, the system worked relatively effectively by late medieval standards.

What problems did the king face in local government?

The most frequent problems of a local nature that the king had to face were the disputes between members of the nobility. During the Wars of the Roses the system of local government had completely collapsed and Edward IV had had to attempt to

Key question
How far did Henry allow individual magnates to build up power in the localities?

Common law courts
Local courts in which cases involving the gentry and peasantry were heard.

rebuild this structure almost from scratch. He had tried to do this in two ways:

- He travelled around the country intervening in disputes and personally hearing cases in the **common law courts**.
- He appointed powerful local magnates to control particular areas.

This system proved quite successful until his death. One of the reasons for this was that Edward had delegated responsibility to only a small number of favoured nobles. These nobles controlled vast areas of land throughout the country, which gave them an enormous amount of power and influence. Generally, Edward had been able to control them but his policy did have its weaknesses, for example, the concentration of power in the hands of a few had:

- led to the creation of over-mighty subjects
- caused discontent among those who had felt overlooked.

Consequently, on the sudden usurpation of Richard III, many seized their opportunity to take authority into their own hands and deliberately chose to ignore royal commands.

Control of the magnates

When Henry VII became king he faced the problem of restraining the individual nobles in the provinces. He saw the strengths in Edward's policy and followed it in principle, but, wherever possible, he stopped individuals building up too much power and he always insisted on their absolute loyalty to the Tudor dynasty. So, although the Stanley family was allowed to enhance its authority and to continue in charge of south Lancashire and Cheshire, control of the south-west of the country was taken away from the Marquess of Dorset after his treachery early in the reign.

Two of Henry's strongest supporters were rewarded with estates which brought with them a considerable amount of local control: Jasper Tudor, Duke of Bedford, became the most influential nobleman in Wales, as did the Earl of Oxford in East Anglia – although their influence never equalled that of Edward's leading nobles.

Supporters of Richard III found it virtually impossible to regain the positions that they had enjoyed under the Yorkists. Although the Earl of Northumberland was allowed to continue in his former role of Lord Lieutenant of the North, his powers were greatly restricted and, on his death in 1489, Henry used the fact that the Percy heir was a minor to replace the earl with Thomas Howard, Earl of Surrey, who had neither land nor influence in the northern counties. Surrey's judgements were therefore likely to be less partial. In addition, as Surrey was hoping to win back the lands and title lost by his father after Bosworth, Henry could expect good service from him. In 1501 the northern families were once again overlooked when Surrey was replaced by a council under the Archbishop of York.

The same pattern emerged in Wales after the deaths of
Jasper Tudor (d. 1495) and the Prince of Wales (d. 1502). Control
was in the hands of a council under the presidency of William
Smyth, Bishop of Coventry and Lichfield, who had no power
base in the Principality. So by the end of his reign Henry was
moving away from the idea of appointing a local magnate to
control a particular region. This prevented the growth of
magnate power and over-mighty subjects in the provinces and in
doing so forged far stronger links between central and local
government.

North/north-east
Henry Percy
Earl of Northumberland

Thomas Howard
Earl of Surrey

**Lancashire, Cheshire
and North Wales**
Thomas Stanley
Earl of Derby

North Midlands
Lord Hastings

Wales and the Marches
Jasper Tudor
Duke of Bedford

**East Midlands and
East Anglia**
John de Vere
Earl of Oxford

West Midlands
George Talbot
Earl of Shrewsbury

South-east
The king and lesser
household men

South-west
Giles, Lord Daubemey
Edward Courtenay
Earl of Devon

Figure 4.1: Noble power blocks post-1485. Henry entrusted power in the localities only to a
small, close circle of noble families. Why did the king appoint the nobles mentioned
to these areas?

Key question
How far did the king centralise royal power in the provinces?

The centralisation of government

Supervision from the centre was the key feature of the exercise of law and government in the localities. This did not mean that Henry made royal progresses around the kingdom involving himself in cases in a personal way as Edward IV had done. Instead, Henry was the central figure directing all operations from London and making his commands felt in three ways:

- through the exploitation of crown lands
- by encouraging more frequent use of the royal council and its offshoots for the settlement of local lawsuits
- by increasing the powers of the JPs.

Henry's more efficient management and exploitation of the crown lands had extended the authority of the monarch to all parts of the country, as well as increasing the income that he received in rents. In developing the role of the royal council and JPs – who owed their offices to the king – Henry was also exerting his control more effectively over the localities. This arrangement worked relatively well under a strong king, who could ensure that his instructions were obeyed and that the local nobility did not develop too much power, or seize the opportunity to pursue their private feuds. Although the problem of keeping the peace had not been completely solved, Henry had gone a long way towards extending his control of the situation by centralising the system of local government.

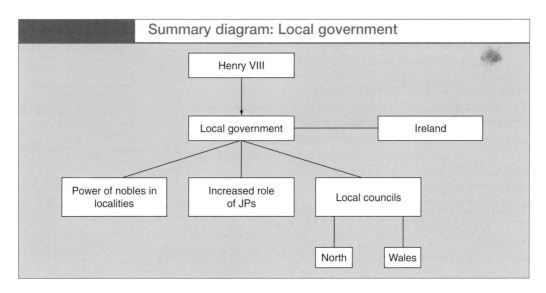

Summary diagram: Local government

Key question
What part had parliament played in medieval government?

4 | Parliament

Parliament before Henry VII

In the fifteenth century the government of England was clearly the responsibility of the king and his council. Parliament played no regular part in the maintenance of law and order. It met only to grant taxes and to pass laws, and it was in this latter role that it was of use to the king in controlling his subjects. Parliament consisted of two Houses – Lords and Commons. The predominance of the Lords can be gauged by where they met – the Lords in a room in the royal palace of Westminster, and the Commons in the nearby chapter house of Westminster Abbey.

The House of Lords
The Lords was made up of two groups: the Lords spiritual (the archbishops, bishops and the heads of the more important monasteries) and the Lords temporal (the peers). Tradition gave the Lords greater authority than the Commons, and it was still the practice in 1485 for important legislation to be introduced first into the House of Lords. However, this was beginning to change before the end of the reign.

The House of Commons
The Commons was composed of MPs chosen by a very limited electorate made up of those who possessed considerable property. Two members were elected to represent each county and borough (a town with a royal charter or letter granting political and economic, usually trading, privileges). The type of men typically sitting in the lower house were the local gentry representing the counties, and merchants and lawyers representing the boroughs. In practice, parliament was the meeting of the king, his councillors and the Lords. The Commons met while the king discussed issues with the Lords, but he only spoke to them about particularly important issues, such as his right to the throne. They communicated with him through the Speaker, elected from among their number, but in fact a royal nominee. Parliament was only summoned when there was a special need to do so, and its meeting normally lasted only a few weeks.

Parliament in Henry VII's reign

Key question
Why did Henry call so few parliaments and why were their meetings so irregular?

The fact that parliament met infrequently is evidence of its limited role in Henry's government (see Table 4.1). In the 24 years of his reign it met on only seven occasions, and five of those were in his first decade as king when he was relatively insecure in his possession of the throne. There were several reasons for this infrequency of meetings:

Key date

Meeting of first parliament: 1485

- Henry did not need to ask for war taxes very often because his foreign policy was based on avoiding expensive campaigns abroad.
- Henry did not wish to strain the loyalty of his subjects by too many requests for grants of money, so he found other ways of filling his treasury.
- Parliament's judicial function as the final court of appeal was now being fulfilled by the subsidiary courts of the Royal Council, such as the Council Learned in the Law.
- Finally, although Henry used parliament for introducing government bills, he did not feel the need to initiate legislation on a large scale. The type of acts most frequently passed were acts of attainder against the king's political opponents. So, from Henry's point of view, parliament was of particular use in helping him subdue the more troublesome magnates.

Table 4.1: Parliamentary meetings under Henry VII

	Date of session	Approximate length of session
1485–6 Parliament	07/11/85–04/03/86	3 months
1487 Parliament	09/11/87–??/12/87	1 month
1489 Parliament	13/01/89–23/02/90	1.5 months
1491 Parliament	17/10/91–04/11/91	0.5 month
1495 Parliament	14/10/95–22/12/95	2 months
1497 Parliament	16/01/97–13/03/97	2 months
1504 Parliament	25/01/04–??/04/04	2.5 months

The king might not have summoned parliament frequently but, by the way he used it, he continued its traditional role as an institution where the most important business of the kingdom was carried out. This is clear not only in the number of attainders against individual nobles that he requested parliament to pass, but in the way he used it to ratify his claim to the throne in 1486.

Legislation was also used to carry out his policies against riots and retaining, and 10 per cent of all statutes dealt with the responsibilities of the JPs and the control of the provinces. Further acts dealt with social discipline, such as that of 1495, which laid down maximum wages and minimum hours of work. Another act instructed vagabonds to be put in the stocks and returned to their original place of residence. Perhaps most importantly, the act of 1504, which forbade **corporations** from making any regulations unless they first had the approval of the king, showed the way in which parliament was being used to emphasise the fact that all power derived from the crown and that there was only one ruler in England.

So, although parliament did not meet on a regular basis during Henry's reign, there was no threat of it ceasing to exist as a political institution. The king used it as and when circumstances demanded, just as his predecessors had done.

Key term

Corporations
Traders and merchants who came together to form an organisation to promote their rights and interests.

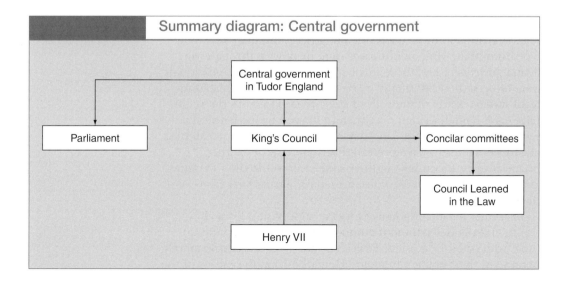

Summary diagram: Central government

5 | The Key Debate

> How far did Henry restore law and order and establish good government?

Many historians have contributed to the analysis of Henry's policies on law and order and whether or not he established good government. These issues remain lively areas of discussion.

Henry largely achieved his ambition of restoring law and order – although by late medieval standards, rather than by those of the present day. However, his way of doing this was different from that of his predecessors. His style of rule was one of personal government; Henry ruled as the master of the most important household in the kingdom. He accomplished this by increasing the authority of the monarchy and by striving to ensure that all his subjects, rich and poor alike, respected and obeyed his will.

He immediately recognised the potential threat posed by the nobility, aware of the way in which they had seized the opportunity to assert their authority under a weak king. He largely succeeded in preventing them from manipulating the law to suit their own purposes by insisting on absolute loyalty from those who gained his confidence and carried out his commands.

However, he did not oust all of them from government, as used to be thought. He was happy to work closely with those nobles he judged to be worthy of his trust, and the practice of entrusting control of the outlying areas of the country to the magnates continued, as, for example, with the Earl of Surrey in the north. But, far more than his predecessors, he strictly enforced the laws against livery and maintenance, ensuring that all obeyed and that no tempting loopholes remained. As a result of his policies, he faced few challenges from over-mighty subjects, and by deliberately refraining from creating many new peers, his magnates became a small, select and loyal group, with those daring to disobey him facing crippling financial penalties.

On the other hand, Henry VII has been criticised because of the small number of cases involving nobles brought before the higher courts. Historians originally interpreted this as a lack of real determination to enforce the law strictly, but later research has shown that, while minor cases were dealt with through the formal process of law, those involving more important individuals were often settled informally to avoid the slow and cumbersome legal system. Many of the rolls of court that exist from the reign have 'case halted' written over them, followed by evidence of a recognisance paid to the king to clear up the matter once and for all. Henry seems to have preferred this method of exerting financial pressure on his mightier subjects to settle their disputes and thousands of such recognisances exist, particularly from later in the reign.

To Henry, personal monarchy meant supervision from the centre and the delegation of authority in the localities only to those who could be trusted. Power was not given to people merely because of their noble parentage. Henry built up the power of the

JP as the most important local official and, in so doing, placed power in the hands of the gentry who, as lesser landowners, were less able to resist the king's will than were their more powerful neighbours. The council became more efficient under Henry's painstaking administration and the responsibilities of its various committees were carefully defined so as to ensure that the king's orders were carried out in all parts of the country.

Of course, there were still problems. Poor communications and the geography of the kingdom often hindered the speedy transmission of the king's instructions. Henry remained reliant on those to whom he delegated his powers, for there was no body of men responsible directly to him. England still did not have a formal police like the Hermandad in Spain, or a standing army as in France. However, compared to the state of the country when he came to the throne, England was relatively law-abiding by the time he died. Strong leadership, increased centralisation and the careful delegation of offices meant that English society was once again generally at peace with itself.

Study Guide: AS Questions

In the style of AQA

Study the following source material and then answer the questions that follow on page 88.

Source A

Adapted from: Edward Hall, Chronicle, *1547.*

Henry VII established in 1485 a Council of wise and politically able men by whose judgement, order and determination the people might be governed fairly according to justice and fairness and that all cases might begin and end there without delay and expense.

Source B

From a letter sent to his government by Milan's ambassador to England, 1496.

Henry VII is feared rather than loved, and this is due to his greed. I asked who ruled him and had control over him. My informant said there was only one man who could do anything and he is Reginald Bray, who controls the king's treasure. The king is very rich, but if chance allowed a lord with royal blood to rebel against him and the king had to fight him he would fare badly because of his greed. The people would abandon Henry VII and treat him as they did King Richard III whom they also abandoned.

Source C

Adapted from: A.J. Pollard, Late Medieval England 1399–1509, *1991.*

Since survival was the key factor of Henry's kingship there remains the question of the extent to which he actively promoted the re-foundation of the monarchy. Henry VII's government was very much concerned with using his councillors. It has been argued by some other historians that his councillors began to separate government from the person of the king in whose name they worked. Those responsible were councillors such as John Morton. The initiative need not have come form the king, but he had the ability to select effective ministers and to see that such a development was in his political interest.

(a) **Use Source A and your own knowledge**
   Explain briefly what was meant by 'a Council' in the context of Henry VII's government of England.   (3 marks)
(b) **Use Source B and your own knowledge**
   Explain how useful Source B is as evidence of Henry VII's authority.   (7 marks)
(c) **Use Sources A, B and C and use your own knowledge**
   'Henry VII's ministers, rather than the king himself, were responsible for the success of his government.' Explain why you agree or disagree with this opinion.   (15 marks)

Source: AQA, 2003

Exam tips
The cross-references are intended to take you straight to the material that will help you to answer the questions.

1. In question **(a)** you should provide a developed explanation of the term and its significance in relation to the context, for example:

    - Refer to the body of men who served Henry directly and helped him govern the kingdom (pages 71–5).
    - Henry used able councillors such as Bray and Morton to help him govern and a key role of the council was to see that justice was both immediate and affordable (pages 71–2).

2. In question **(b)** you have to understand what is being said in the source and, for purposes of utility, who is saying it in order to evaluate its usefulness. You must consider its strengths and weaknesses, for example:

    - It was written by a foreigner who may not have fully grasped the nature of Henry's government in that he had no obvious favourite (page 98).
    - It was written during Henry's lifetime by someone who knew him.
    - Henry's authority extended further than the source suggests, which is concerned, in the main, with his financial policies (page 82).

3. In question **(c)** you should evaluate the extent to which the king's ministers were responsible for the success of government rather than any contribution made by the king himself. For example:

- You must try to make effective use of the sources together with your own knowledge in order to provide a balanced answer.
- You should provide a range of reasons in addition to the work of the king's ministers, e.g. Henry had the power to appoint and dismiss ministers, decisions could only be taken and ratified with the king's consent.
- You should draw on the information contained in the sources together with some appreciation of the reliability of those responsible for expressing their opinions. For example differentiate between the largely subjective comments of contemporaries and near-contemporaries in A and B and the more objective opinion expressed by the historian in C. It is important to remember that a substantiated conclusion must be reached showing judgement.

In the style of Edexcel

Study Sources 1–5 below and answer questions (a)–(e) that follow.

Source 1

From: Polydore Vergil, History of England, *written in 1513.*

Henry VII established a Council in his household by whose opinion all things should be justly and rightly governed and causes brought to it to be decided without the bitterness of lawsuits. And for this Council, he chose men renowned for their shrewdness, loyalty and reliability, John, Earl of Oxford; Jasper, Duke of Bedford; Thomas Stanley, Earl of Derby … John Morton, Bishop of Ely; Richard Fox; Edward Poynings … and he chose other wise men to council for specific business among whom were Rhys ap Thomas, a Welshman; Thomas Grey, Marquis of Dorset, a good and prudent man; George Talbot, Earl of Shrewsbury, wise and moderate in all things; Thomas, Earl of Ormond, an Irishman; William Say, a prominent knight; Thomas Earl of Surrey, a man of great wisdom, reliability and loyalty.

Source 2

Part of a letter written by a merchant, Giovanni de Bebulcho to the government of Milan. The letter records a conversation he had with a Florentine merchant who had recently arrived from England in July 1496.

I asked him about English affairs. He said that the king is more feared than loved. I asked who had influence with the king. He said there was only one who can do anything, and he is named Reginald Bray, who controls the king's treasure.

Source 3

From: a case brought before the Court of Requests by Thomas Lacey, who held his lands directly from the king, in 1497.

On the Monday before the Feast of All Saints [31st October 1496], John Saville, accompanied by about 80 armed and ill-disposed persons, came to my town of Southowrom. Then by force they took oxen, cattle and horses over 90 in number and drove them out of my land to Saville's property at Illingworth where he penned them up. Upon this I sent to the sheriff for help against Saville for his wrongful taking of the animals. However, Saville refused to give up the animals but kept them in clear contempt of the law.

Source 4

Sir Reginald Bray, one of Henry VII's leading advisers, portrayed in a stained glass window at Malvern Priory.

Source 5

From: J. Hunt and C. Towle, Henry VII, *published in 1998.*

How well did Henry govern? If you compare the situation before and after his reign you have to say that he had done well. Law and order was [*sic.*] established; the budget was in surplus; trade was flourishing, and with it the merchant classes; nobles were no longer a danger to national order; the Church was less corrupt than it had been, though still far from perfect; ordinary people could be confident that their lives would not be disrupted by the kind of disorder which their forefathers had suffered.

(a) **Study Source 1**

What can you learn from Source 1 about the men on whom Henry VII relied for advice in his Council? (6 marks)

(b) **Use your own knowledge**

Use your own knowledge to explain the significance of the 'Court of Star Chamber'. (10 marks)

(c) **Study Sources 3 and 5**

How far do Sources 3 and 5 disagree about the state of law and order in England during the reign of Henry VII?

(10 marks)

(d) **Study Sources 2 and 4**

How useful are these two sources to an historian studying the importance of Reginald Bray in the reign of Henry VII?

(10 marks)

(e) **Study Sources 3 and 5 and use your own knowledge**

Do you agree with the view that Henry's government was popular and effective? Explain your answer, using the sources and your own knowledge. (24 marks)

Exam tips

The cross-references are intended to take you straight to the material that will help you answer the questions.

1. The answer to question **(a)** is to be found entirely within Source 1. You have to show that you have understood the content of the source. You do not have to use your own knowledge. You must remember to explain what the source implies or infers about the men on whom the king relied in Council. Keep your answer to the point, for example:

   • The Council consisted of nobles, gentry and clergymen.
   • The majority of the councillors listed were of the nobility.

2. In question **(b)** you must use your own knowledge to explain the significance of the Court of Star Chamber, for example:

   • The Star Chamber was an important part of the machinery of justice (pages 72–3).
   • The Court enabled Henry to discipline members of the nobility and gentry.

3. In question **(c)** you have to understand what is being said in Sources 3 and 5. Evaluate the extent to which the Source 3 disagrees with the view of the historians in Source 5. Take care to discuss its limitations, for example.

   • The references to law breaking and disorder clearly contradict the views expressed in Source 5.
   • The references to the apparent ineffectiveness of the sheriff and to the brazen behaviour of the law-breaker may also be used to disagree with the views expressed in Source 5.

4. In question **(d)** you have to focus on the key word 'useful' and suggest ways in which an historian might find Sources 2 and 5 useful in studying the importance of Reginald Bray. Be mindful of who has written and/or commissioned the source and why, for example:

   - Source 2 suggests that Bray was by far the most important of the king's close advisers.
   - Source 5 suggests that Bray was important enough to be commemorated in glass at Malvern Priory.
   - On the other hand, you might argue that the opinion expressed in Source 2 is that of a foreigner who may have obtained his information by rumour and hearsay. Also the stained glass depiction of Bray does not support the view that he was one of Henry's most important councillors, only that he was a well-known and wealthy local landowner.

5. Question **(e)** carries the greatest number of marks, so deserves the greatest amount of time devoted to it. You have to recall your own knowledge in order to discuss the extent to which Henry's government was effective and popular. You must assess the effectiveness and popularity of Henry's government by reference to the sources, the contents of which are there to help you. (You must resist the temptation to copy the source content but specific quotation is permissible if it is used to support a point you are trying to make.) You must show your awareness of the fact that not everyone would be happy and contented, no matter how effective the king's government proved to be. You should show how Henry's success in:

   - ending the Wars of the Roses (pages 11–18)
   - establishing the dynasty through marriage and by having heirs (page 3)
   - increasing trade and political stability (pages 124–30), which contributed to making his government generally popular and effective.

   You should round off your answer by offering an opinion in respect of how far you agree or disagree with the question.

In the style of OCR

(a) To what extent had government changed under Henry VII between 1485 and 1509? (45 marks)

(b) How effective was Henry VII's government? (45 marks)

Exam tips

The cross-references are intended to take you straight to the material that will help you to answer the questions.

1. In question **(a)** you should be able to clearly evaluate and explain the extent to which government changed during Henry VII's reign. Your evaluation should be balanced. You should also be able to come to a substantiated conclusion where an overall judgement can be offered, for example:

    - Henry relied on traditional methods of government so he did not innovate but adapted the system he inherited, for example the functions and duties of the Council did not change; institutions such as parliament did not change; the concept of kingship did not change; Henry enforced his traditional powers; the nobility remained influential in local government (pages 78–82).
    - On the other hand, Henry reduced the size of the Council to make it more efficient and he employed more gentry than nobility to serve as his advisers; the nobility became less important in central government; the organisation of government became more effective (pages 71–5).

2. In question **(b)** the examiner is testing your ability to analyse and evaluate, therefore it is important to remember that marks will be awarded both for the factual content of your answer and for the analytical skills you display. You should compare the situation at the beginning and end of Henry's reign to see if there was any change and make an overall judgement. You should provide a balanced answer showing clearly, with examples, where the government was at its most and least efficient, for example:

    - Henry's government improved law and order but its greatest success was probably in finance (pages 94–5).
    - The government contributed to the establishment of the dynasty by promoting peace and stability.

    On the other hand:

    - The government of the outlying regions of the kingdom was not so effective, e.g. in Ireland where the pretender Simnel was crowned king and in the North when rebellion broke out in Yorkshire (pages 30–1).
    - It mishandled the collection of taxation, which led to the Cornish rebellion (pages 31–3).
    - It is worth noting that the government's ruthless efficiency under Empson and Dudley led to it becoming unpopular towards the end of Henry's reign (pages 74–5).

5 Seeking Solvency: Henry's Financial Policy

POINTS TO CONSIDER
Solvency and financial security were essential if Henry VII was to remain as king. This chapter will examine how Henry attempted to become financially secure in order to consolidate the dynasty through looking at the following themes:

- Henry's financial aims
- The changes made to the administration of the financial system to achieve those aims
- How the crown was financed through ordinary and extraordinary revenue

Key dates

1 | Henry's Financial Aims

Henry has been credited with being 'the best businessman ever to sit upon the English throne', and on his death he was described as the 'richest lord that is now known in the world' by Francis Bacon. These opinions are exaggerated: he died **solvent**, but that was all. However, both his contemporaries and later historians have concentrated on emphasising his financial success.

In spite of his lack of experience in government, Henry was acutely aware of the importance of strong finances if he was to remain safely on his throne. He told Henry Wyatt, one of his Councillors, that 'the Kings my predecessors, weakening their treasure, have made themselves servants to their subjects'. His own usurpation of the crown meant there was always the possibility of others putting forward their own claim. The availability of revenue together with financial stability was essential if he was to be able to raise an army to defeat them.

Key question
Why did Henry consider it to be so important to improve the crown's financial position?

Solvent
Financially sound and without debt.

Key term

Key terms

Treasury
Held the king's wealth in money and goods.

Live of their own
Kings were expected to live within their financial means.

Henry VII did not feel secure unless he was rich: he could use his wealth to reward loyal service, bribe potential opponents and fund armies if necessary. Therefore, a full **treasury** helps to explain why he was successful in quelling the rebellions against him. It helped him to consolidate the dynasty because if the succession was still challenged at the time of his death, a full treasury would provide his son with the resources to fight to retain his throne. This is why Henry was so keen to reorganise the financial administration because he believed that a wealthy king was a secure king, one who was better able to finance his way out of trouble. However, Henry was well aware that his determination to make the collection of revenue more efficient would encounter opposition from those who would be expected to pay.

Key question
What constraints did Henry face in the management of his financial affairs?

Financial constraints

One of the limitations facing Henry in the management of his financial affairs was that throughout the middle ages English kings had been expected to '**live of their own**'. They formally swore to do so at their coronation. This meant that they had to manage on the regular income that came to them annually as monarchs and landowners (see pages 100–6).

Henry knew that any proposal to raise money from new sources would arouse suspicion and probably provoke opposition. The king could not ask parliament for a grant (additional taxation) except in unusual circumstances, such as war. There was always the fear that, if additional direct taxes were demanded frequently, rebellion might soon follow. This is why, when it came to financial matters, Henry did not innovate. He preferred to follow the example set by his Yorkist predecessors who showed that the existing revenues could be expanded sufficiently to give him the financial strength he needed (see page 10).

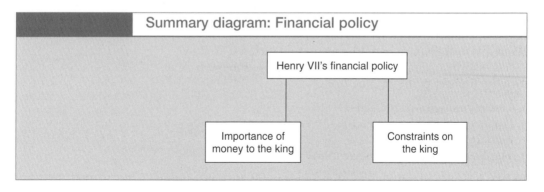

Summary diagram: Financial policy

Key question
What were the main financial institutions?

2 | Financial Administration

The Exchequer
Since the twelfth century the centre of the crown's financial administration had been the Exchequer. This had two functions:

- to receive, store and pay out money
- to audit the accounts.

To organise this department and prevent fraud and embezzlement there was a complex hierarchy of officials. Although it worked in an honest and reliable fashion for the time, it did have flaws. The system was slow and cumbersome, outstanding sums often taking years to collect, and audits being equally behind time. It was because of this that the Yorkist kings had developed the Chamber as their financial department.

The Chamber

The Chamber was a more informal and flexible system than the Exchequer, partly because it had not been involved in royal finance for very long. It had originated from the accounting system used on the estates of the great nobles who appointed officials called **receivers** and **auditors** from within their household to run certain groups of their estates, particularly in their absence. Edward IV had been familiar with this practice on the Yorkist estates, so when he became king in 1461, he applied it to the royal estates. He had chosen to use the King's Chamber, the innermost part of the king's household, to handle his finances in an attempt to exert more personal control over what happened.

In the first two years of his reign Henry VII had neither the experience nor the time to continue this practice – a decision that he must later have regretted – so the Exchequer resumed its control of royal finances. However, as early as 1487 Henry admitted that in focusing so intensely on his own security, he had neglected to take adequate care of his estates and that they had 'greatly fallen into decay'. The accounts bear witness to this. In Richard III's reign they had brought in £25,000 per annum, but by 1486 this had declined to £12,000.

Key terms

Receivers
Financial officials who collected and stored money on behalf of the king.

Auditors
Financial officials who counted and wrote down the figures in an account book.

Reorganising the royal household

From 1487 Henry gradually began to restore the Chamber system to its former position as the most important institution of financial administration. By the late 1490s it was once again the centre of royal finance, handling an annual turnover well in excess of £100,000 (about £4 million in today's money). It dealt with the transfer of all revenue from:

Key question
How did Henry reorganise the royal household?

- Crown lands (see pages 100–1)
- Profits of justice (see pages 102–3)
- Feudal dues (see page 102)
- The French pension (see page 105).

In fact, it dealt with all sources of income except **customs duties** and the accounts of the sheriffs (the officials responsible for the maintenance of law and order in the shires). These remained under the control of the Exchequer because their collection involved detailed information and a complex organisation of officers and records not available to the **Treasurer of the Chamber**. Richard III (1483–5) had laid the basis for the reform of the financial administration and Henry was able to continue this with the help of his officials, many of whom had been trained under the Yorkist regime.

Key terms

Customs duties
Taxes imposed on imported goods.

Treasurer of the Chamber
Chief financial official responsible for the king's money.

The Privy Chamber

The development of the Chamber into the national treasury from 1487 automatically led to further reorganisation within the household, from where the Chamber had originated. The department that increased most in importance was the king's 'Privy [private] Chamber', made up of his personal household servants. This now took over the administration of the royal household as well as taking care of Henry's private expenditure, formerly a responsibility of the Chamber.

The chief officer of the Privy Chamber, the Groom of the Stool, became second in importance to the Treasurer of the Chamber, and lesser household officials, such as **Gentlemen of the Bedchamber, grooms and ushers**, found that new opportunities for promotion were open to them. The transformation of the Privy Chamber is important because it continued to play a vital role in Tudor government throughout the sixteenth century, and many Tudor ministers rose from its ranks.

The head of the financial system, at least in theory, was the Treasurer of England, but he had long been merely a figurehead and the office was traditionally given to an important noble as an honorary position. The only holders of the office for the whole of Henry's reign were Lord Dynham (1485–1501) and the Earl of Surrey (1501–22). In practice, the Treasurer of the Chamber had become the chief financial officer of the crown. Under Henry VII, this position was held by two of the king's most loyal and efficient servants, Sir Thomas Lovell (1485–92) and Sir John Heron (1492–1521). The main advantage of the Chamber system to the king was that it gave him much closer control over his finances since Henry worked alongside both men, checking the accounts himself and leaving his signature on them as proof of their accuracy.

Key term

Gentlemen of the Bedchamber, grooms and ushers
Titles given to the personal servants of the king. Those who attended him every day.

A page from the book of Chamber Receipts (August 1492), showing the king's signature against the entries of moneys received by Master Bray and the Abbot of Reading. Why did Henry take a keen interest in financial matters?

Profile: Sir Reginald Bray 1440–1503

Key question
How significant was Bray's contribution to the success of Henry's financial policy?

1460s – Served as steward of the household of Sir Henry Stafford, second husband of Margaret, mother of Henry Tudor

1485 – Knighted by Henry VII

1492 – Appointed to Henry VII's council as chief financial adviser
– Appointed paymaster-general of the army that Henry took to France

1494 – Appointed high-steward of Oxford University

1497 – Helped defeat and disperse the Cornish rebels on Blackheath in London

1503 – Died

The revived financial administration demanded loyalty, efficiency and integrity from the officials in charge. Henry chose his officials carefully and was well served by them. His most trusted adviser in financial matters was his friend Sir Reginald Bray, the Chancellor of the Duchy of Lancaster.

Bray had come to Henry's attention as an important member of his mother's (Margaret Beaufort) household. He sat in parliament and was a valued councillor, but it was as Chancellor of the Duchy of Lancaster, in charge of administering one of the richest, most efficient and, therefore, most important groups of royal estates in the country, that Henry became aware of his administrative skills. His real power depended not so much on his official position as on the fact that he held the trust and confidence of the king – thus illustrating once again the personal role of the monarch in government.

Bray had been responsible for successfully restoring effective estate management in the Duchy, which had been disrupted by the civil disorder of the 1450s and by Richard III's seizure of power. It was for this reason that Henry entrusted him with the task of introducing new methods of auditing the accounts. Although he held no formal office in either the Chamber or Exchequer, Bray became the king's chief financial adviser (he was sometimes described as the 'under-treasurer of England').

Bray did not work in isolation. He co-operated closely with both Lovell and Heron, and other household officials, making the system more efficient by holding frequent meetings to discuss and examine the Chamber accounts. According to Giovanni de Bebulcho, an Italian merchant, Bray, 'who controls the king's treasure', was the only man who really had any influence over Henry. Bray's death in 1503 hit the king hard but he found in Sir Robert Southwell a worthy successor. Southwell had been one of the king's most efficient auditors and he was promoted by Bray to become his assistant. Like Bray, Southwell's talent lay in offering the king advice on financial matters and in devising new and more efficient methods of collecting and accounting for money paid into the royal treasury.

Sir Reginald Bray depicted in stained glass in a transept window in Great Malvern Priory. How far can Sir Reginald Bray's depiction in stained glass in Great Malvern Priory be taken as proof of his fame and importance?

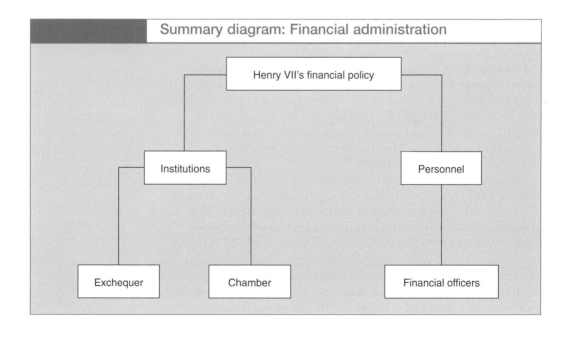

Summary diagram: Financial administration

Henry VII's financial policy

Institutions

Personnel

Exchequer

Chamber

Financial officers

3 | The Financial Resources of the Crown

Key question
Where did the money come from?

Historians frequently make a distinction between two separate types of revenue that rulers received at this time. These were 'ordinary' revenue and 'extraordinary' revenue.

- Ordinary revenue came in every year, although in different amounts, from crown lands and custom duties, but also included the profits of justice (fines) and feudal dues on lands held in return for avoiding military service. It was largely on the income from ordinary revenue that kings were expected to 'live of their own'.
- Extraordinary revenue came from the subject's obligation to help the king in time of need. By the fifteenth century, this usually meant taxation **levied** in parliament, which came in the form of a 'grant' that the king had to request from his subjects. Less frequently, it could also be money that came to the king as feudal overlord, a right that belonged to any feudal lord; this was known as a 'feudal aid' and was levied on specific occasions. For example, if the king was captured and held to ransom, he could demand an aid to raise the money necessary to obtain his release. It could also be money raised by borrowing from his richer subjects in an emergency, or gifts from other rulers, often granted as part of a favourable peace treaty. The Church, too, contributed, in the form of clerical taxes, towards the financial well-being of the kingdom.

Key terms

Levies
Money raised by order of the king.

Escheat
Where a landholder died without heirs, his lands passed by right to the king.

Ordinary revenue

Key question
How successfully did Henry exploit the different forms of ordinary revenue available to him?

Crown lands

The most important way in which Henry increased his ordinary revenue was by maximising the income from crown lands. This was partly because they were collected more efficiently, but also because Henry, unlike Edward IV, did not grant a large proportion of them to his family and supporters – he thus retained the profits from them for himself.

Coming to the throne at the end of the Wars of the Roses, Henry inherited all the lands that had belonged to the houses of York and Lancaster, including the Earldoms of Richmond, March and Warwick, the Duchy of Lancaster and the Principality of Wales. On the deaths of his uncle and his wife, their lands reverted to him as well. He also further enriched the crown through **escheats** and attainders.

Henry pursued a different policy towards his lands from that of Edward IV. This was partly due to his personal circumstances. He was lucky in having few relatives who expected to benefit from his territorial acquisitions. He had no brothers; his uncle, Jasper Tudor, died in 1495, and his elder son, Arthur, in 1502. This left only Prince Henry requiring provision. Henry had no obvious favourites, nor was he inclined to shower honours on his supporters. Therefore, on his death, the crown lands were more extensive than they had ever been. Efficient management, a thrifty nature and good fortune meant that the annual income

Key date

Act of Resumption:
1486

Key term

Act of Resumption
An act whereby the
king takes back land
granted as rewards
by previous
monarchs.

from crown lands had increased from £29,000 on the death of
Richard III in 1485 to £42,000 in 1509.

Henry recognised the importance of land from the start,
encouraging his first parliament of 1485–6 to pass the **Act of
Resumption**, which recovered for the crown all properties
granted away since 1455. However, having stated his claim, he
did not take back all the estates involved because he did not wish
to antagonise the majority of noble families affected by the act.
Henry knew that if he was to consolidate the dynasty he must try
to gain the support of the nobility by showing them he was
prepared to compromise. For example, he allowed the Marquis of
Dorset to keep some of the lands granted to him by Richard III.

The Duchy of Lancaster

The Duchy of Lancaster, which had come to the crown with
Henry IV in 1399, played a key role in transforming and
updating the administration of the rest of the crown lands. It is a
good example of how Henry VII fully capitalised on this source
of income.

Unlike other groups of crown lands, the Duchy had its own
organisation centred around its Chancellor and it had adopted
the new methods of estate management long before most
noblemen or the king. At the beginning of Henry's reign it
brought in £650 per year to the Chamber, but by 1509 this had
increased 10-fold under the skilful management of Sir Reginald
Bray. The accounts were rigorously checked by the king and the
receivers, and the chief financial officers for the individual estates
were encouraged to make ever bigger profits.

Customs duties

At the beginning of Henry's reign customs duties on imported
goods made up the largest part of the king's income, but by 1509
they had been overtaken by the revenue from crown lands.
However, customs duties were still providing a third of the
ordinary revenue. In the late fifteenth century the principal duties
levied were on wool, leather, cloth and wine, but many of these
(such as that on cloth) had not changed since 1347.

Under Edward IV, the average annual yield had increased
owing to his encouragement of trade and a tighter
administration, which cut down on fraud at all levels. Henry
followed his example successfully by blocking many of the
loopholes in the system. For example, from 1487, merchants
involved in coastal trading, carrying merchandise from one
English port to another, were required to produce a certificate
from the first port specifying the duties paid. In 1496 Henry
tried to reduce some of the privileges enjoyed by foreign
merchants, e.g. immunity from English taxation. Twice during his
reign he updated the Book of Rates of customs duties to be paid
in London.

However, despite Henry's efforts, income from customs did not
greatly increase. The average annual receipts were about £33,000
for the first 10 years of the reign and about £40,000 thereafter.

Smuggling seems to have continued, in spite of stricter control, and even Henry could not manipulate international trade entirely to his whim: it was dependent on the fragile and changing relationships between all the European powers.

Feudal dues

Another part of the crown's income was the feudal dues, paid by those who held land from the king in return for avoiding military service. As the greatest feudal lord, the king was owed certain obligations by his tenants-in-chief (those holding their land directly from the king), just as they in turn were owed the same duties by their tenants. These included wardship, **marriage**, livery and the fine known as '**relief**'. Henry was determined to enforce these traditional rights to the full and to extract the maximum income possible from them. Initially, the proceeds from wardship and marriage were small, amounting to only £350 in 1487, but after 1503 a special officer (the Master of the King's Wards) was appointed to supervise them, and by 1507 the annual income had risen to £6000.

Key date

Office of the Master of Wards established: 1503

Key terms

Marriage
The royal right to arrange the marriage, for a fee, of heirs and heiresses.

Relief
A payment the king received on the transfer of lands through inheritance.

Profits of justice

As monarch Henry was head of the judicial system and was therefore entitled to its profits. The law courts yielded income in two ways:

- The fees paid by those involved in a court case for the legal writ or summons necessary for any case to begin. This provided the king with a continuous and not inconsiderable income.
- The fines levied by the courts as punishment. The amount raised by fines was irregular because it depended on the number of cases heard in court, but the sums involved were often considerable.

After Henry's death it was widely claimed by contemporaries that he had perverted the legal system by charging his leading subjects with crimes merely in order to profit from the fines that could then be imposed on them. It appears that these allegations were largely unfounded. Certainly, legal fines made a significant contribution to Henry's income but, although high, they were exacted mainly for serious crimes. There is no evidence to suggest that most of the culprits were anything other than guilty of the offences with which they were charged.

However, he did ensure that most criminal acts, including treason, were punished by fines rather than by imprisonment or execution. This brought him much more profit, as happened with his treatment of the rebels after the insurrection in Cornwall in 1497 (see pages 31–2).

Even in lesser cases, Henry appears to have put financial gain first and he did exploit the system. The receipts from sales of pardons for murder and other cases that still survive are evidence of this. The example of the Earl of Northumberland, who was ordered to pay £10,000 for ravishing a royal ward, was probably a way of compensating for the income that Henry had lost with the ending of the Earl's minority.

Another type of fine that the king used as punishment against opponents was that of attainder. Sir William Stanley brought the crown £9000 in cash (in income from his lands) and £1000 per annum after his treason in 1495. There was only one parliament during the reign that omitted to pass any attainders and the highest number in any session was 51.

Key question
How successfully did Henry exploit the different forms of extraordinary revenue available to him?

Extraordinary revenue

Parliamentary grants

Extraordinary revenue was money which came to the crown on particular occasions and therefore with no regularity. It arose from the obligation of the king's subjects to help him when the national interest was threatened. By the later middle ages, the main form of extraordinary revenue was a sum of money granted by parliament. Henry did not misuse this right. Like his Tudor descendants, he was reluctant to tax unless absolutely necessary. This was because, during the fifteenth century, the Lancastrian kings had encountered difficulties with parliament which, realising it had a bargaining position, had demanded restrictions on the king's power in exchange for grants of money. Henry was therefore cautious in his demands from parliament. However, he did request financial assistance in 1487 to pay for the battle of Stoke, in 1489 to go to war against the French, and in 1496 to defend the throne against attack from the Scots and Perkin Warbeck (see pages 33–9).

Historians have accused Henry of cheating his subjects by raising money for wars that never actually took place, as in 1496. Certainly, Henry received the grant from parliament after the initial invasion of the Scots had failed to cross the border, but it could be argued that the money was still needed as the attack might have been renewed at any time. In the event, there was no further trouble from Scotland, but some of the money was used to suppress a rebellion in Cornwall.

Types of taxation

The usual type of tax levied was a national assessment. This was a fifteenth (in the countryside) and a tenth (in the towns) of the value of a subject's movable goods. Several of these grants could be levied by one session of parliament, depending on how much the king needed.

This was not really satisfactory as it was based on town and county assessments that were centuries out of date, and which therefore did not tap anything approaching all the available taxable wealth of the country. So in 1489, when he needed £100,000 to finance the French war, Henry tried another method – a form of income tax, a practice tried unsuccessfully by Edward IV in 1472. This directly assessed subsidy was viewed with suspicion and hostility in parliament, which insisted that no precedents were to be set and no returns were to be made to any court of record. Parliament was clearly trying to ensure that no records would be kept for future use or reference. However, this was largely a failure as only about a third of the anticipated amount was actually collected. As a result, in 1496 Henry returned to the established method of taxation, and it was left to his successors to develop more efficient systems of direct taxation.

Loans

The king could also rely on loans from his richer subjects in times of emergency. In 1496 Henry was desperate for extra cash to defeat Warbeck and the Scots (see pages 36–9). He appealed to his land-holding subjects for financial support. Such requests were virtually impossible to decline, even though they were traditionally in the form of 'agreements'. Henry seems to have asked for only modest sums, around £10,000, and there is no evidence of any resentment, probably as most of the loans appear to have been repaid. In truth, Henry had little choice but to repay them because those subjects who were owed money by the king were more likely to support a rival claimant to the throne.

Benevolences

Rather a different matter was the **benevolence**, a kind of forced loan. This had been introduced by Edward IV in 1475 when he was preparing to invade France. It was a general tax more far-reaching than the fifteenth and tenth. Subjects were asked to contribute to the king's expenses as a sign of their goodwill towards him at a time of crisis. If not overused, it was an effective way of raising money.

In 1491 Henry raised a forced loan when he intended to take his army across the Channel to protect Brittany from French aggression; this produced £48,500, a considerable amount when compared with the sums yielded by direct taxation. **Royal Commissioners** were stringent in its collection. One lady offering only £5 of the £20 deemed appropriate for her to contribute was threatened with being summoned before the king's council.

Clerical taxes

Henry received quite substantial sums from the Church, although smaller amounts than those collected after the Reformation, when, in 1534, the Church came under the control of the state. On several occasions, usually when parliament made a grant, the **convocations** followed suit with their own contributions. In 1489 they voted £25,000 towards the cost of the French war.

Henry also made money from **simony**, charging £300 for the Archdeaconry of Buckingham on one occasion. Like many of his predecessors, the king kept bishoprics vacant for many months before making new appointments so that he could pocket the revenue in the meantime. Due to a rash of deaths among the bishops in the last years of the reign, Henry received over £6000 per annum in this way. However, he did not exploit this method as much as some of his contemporaries in other countries such as France or Spain; whereas they often prolonged vacancies for

Key terms

Benevolence
A type of forced loan that would not be repaid.

Royal Commissioners
Local officials directly appointed by the king to see to his affairs.

Convocation
A kind of parliament for the Church in which representatives of the clergy met to discuss clerical matters.

Simony
The selling of church appointments.

Key term

Diocese
Territory and
churches over which
a bishop has
control.

years, he rarely left a **diocese** without a bishop for more than 12 months.

Feudal obligations

Another type of extraordinary revenue was connected with feudal obligations. As the chief feudal lord, the king had the right to demand feudal aid on special occasions, such as the knighting of his eldest son and the marriage of his eldest daughter. He was also able to levy distraint of knighthood, the medieval practice of forcing those with an annual income of £40 or more to become a mounted knight to fight for the king in time of war. Henry fully exploited these rights, even receiving £30,000 in 1504 for the knighting of Prince Arthur 15 years earlier, although he had died in 1502, and for the marriage of the Princess Margaret to the King of Scotland, which had also taken place in 1502.

The French pension

Key date

Signing of the Treaty
of Étaples: 1492

As part of the Treaty of Étaples in 1492 (see pages 143–4) Henry negotiated a pension from the King of France, a similar policy to that followed by Edward IV in the Treaty of Picquigny in 1475. In practice, the pensions were a bribe offered by their French counterparts so that the English armies would be removed from French soil. Henry was promised £159,000 to compensate him for the cost of the war, a sum to be paid in annual amounts of about £5000.

Bonds and recognisances

Key question
Did Henry
unnecessarily exploit
bonds and
recognisances?

Henry also exploited another source of extraordinary revenue through bonds and recognisances. In general terms this was the practice of subjects paying a sum of money to the crown as a guarantee of their future good behaviour. However, there was a subtle difference between the two.

Bonds

Bonds were written obligations in which people promised to perform some specific action on pain of paying money if they failed to carry out their promise. Bonds had long been used as a condition for the appointment of officials, particularly customs staff, but in the later fifteenth century their use was extended to private individuals as a way of keeping the peace and ensuring loyalty to the government.

Recognisances

Recognisances were formal acknowledgements of actual debts or other obligations that already existed. Under Henry, recognisances became the normal way of ensuring payment of legal debts owed to the crown. Such was Henry's personal interest in such matters that none was issued without his explicit agreement. Almost immediately after Bosworth, he demanded a recognisance of £10,000 from Viscount Beaumont of Powicke and a similar sum from the Earl of Westmorland as guarantees of their loyalty in the future.

Most of these commitments entered into with the king were for routine transactions, such as those with merchants who postponed payment of customs duties. Others were somewhat dubious, for example, recognisances to cover the release of criminals from prison or for the pardon of murderers. At its best, and certainly in those early insecure years of his reign, this financial screw was an effective way of restoring law and order and the evidence shows that, in most cases, it brought in the revenue Henry wanted.

Results of the policy

In the first decade of the reign, 191 bonds were collected. In Henry's later years even more bonds were gathered. The growth in the activity is well reflected by the fact that the receipts from bonds rose from £3000 in 1493 to £35,000 in 1505. Those who fell behind in these payments were hounded by the king's officials, particularly those from the Council Learned in the Law (see pages 74–5), which was made responsible for bonds and recognisances. The Council became greatly feared because of the efficiency of two of its officials, Richard Empson and Edmund Dudley, in pursuing defaulters. Indeed, after Dudley's arrival, the records of the council trebled.

Out of 62 noble families in existence during Henry's reign, 46 were at one time or another financially at his mercy: seven were under attainder, 36 were bound by recognisances or obligations, and three by other means. It is from such evidence that some historians have concluded that Henry's main aim in using bonds and recognisances was to fill his coffers, and so his reputation for greed grew, particularly in the later years of the reign.

However, the receipts tell us more than this, as in the case of the Earl of Northumberland. Dudley recorded that Henry intended to make him pay only £2000, although he was originally made to promise much more. This suggests that Henry's chief concern was to threaten financial ruin in order to maintain his

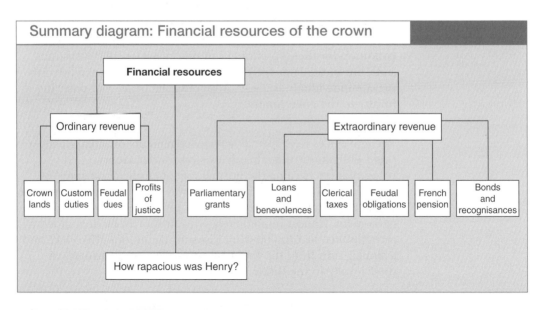

Summary diagram: Financial resources of the crown

Financial resources

Ordinary revenue — Extraordinary revenue

Crown lands | Custom duties | Feudal dues | Profits of justice | Parliamentary grants | Loans and benevolences | Clerical taxes | Feudal obligations | French pension | Bonds and recognisances

How rapacious was Henry?

subjects' loyalty rather than merely increasing his income. Therefore, one might argue that Henry's financial policies were designed to consolidate the dynasty and bolster his security.

4 | The Key Debate

Was Henry unnecessarily greedy or just ruthlessly efficient?

Many historians have contributed to the analysis of Henry's financial policies and whether he was unnecessarily greedy or just ruthlessly efficient. These issues remain lively areas of discussion.

Henry's reputation for being greedy is based largely on what Polydore Vergil, a **papal tax collector** in England from 1502, wrote in his *Anglica Historia*. When describing the later years of the reign Vergil wrote that the people 'considered they were suffering not on account of their own sins but on account of the greed of their monarch'. There is perhaps more to this than greed. After the death of Prince Arthur, in 1502, followed shortly afterwards by that of Queen Elizabeth, Henry may have felt that the security of his dynasty was at risk. His policy of increasingly binding his noble subjects to him financially was an attempt to avoid this.

Nevertheless, it was a policy fraught with danger for, in accumulating this money from the nobility, Henry ran the risk of alienating the very people he would need if his throne were threatened. It was a point noted by a merchant from Florence recently returned from England, who said that 'The king is very powerful in money, but if fortune allowed some lord of the blood to rise and he had to take the field, he would fare badly owing to his avarice; his people would abandon him'.

No-one can dispute that Henry made the most extensive use of the means at his disposal to improve his financial position. Compared to earlier and later monarchs, he appears to have been obsessed with making money. Yet, as the lavishness of his court shows clearly, he was not the miserly king of myth. His 'obsession' may have been due, in part, to the relative poverty of his early years in exile. In the words of his celebrated modern biographer, S.B. Chrimes, 'no man has ascended the throne with such a lack of financial experience and resources as did Henry'. His methods were certainly tenacious and he became the subject of scrutiny by succeeding generations. Yet that he worked so hard and so successfully to improve the monarch's financial independence was to England's advantage, in ensuring a continuation of strong and stable government.

Historians continue to argue over how grasping Henry's financial extortions were. The main conclusions they have reached are:

- There was nothing unusual in the collection of Henry's ordinary revenue and, if anything, it could be described as casual, except over customs duties.

Key term

Papal tax collector Official appointed by the Pope in Rome to collect revenue owed to the Church in countries such as England.

- On the other hand, it is clear that with his extraordinary revenue he was energetic in enforcing his feudal prerogatives and that he did stretch them beyond what could be considered a reasonable limit. For example, it is thought that with bonds and recognisances Henry was guilty of exploiting the system shamelessly, especially after 1502.

Although his policy can be defended in part by arguing that the full sum due was rarely collected, receipts show that the amounts received were still unreasonably high. This view was supported by the confession made by Edmund Dudley shortly after he was arrested and before his execution for treason on the accession of Henry VIII. In this statement, he cited 84 cases where he believed people had been unjustly forced to pay. He did not deliberately intend to discredit Henry, but to make restitution to those 'persons by his grace wronged contrary to the order of his laws' and so to 'win help and relief for the dead king's soul'.

These examples, and others like them, do seem to condemn the king because it seems that Dudley had no reason to lie at this stage. Perhaps Henry provided the final evidence against himself when he made provision in his will for a committee to investigate 'any complaint … or any wrong to have been done … by us or by our commandment'. Henry VIII certainly did nothing to challenge the exaggerated descriptions of his father's financial exactions that appeared later. This has only added to Henry VII's reputation for greed.

It is difficult to be accurate about the total annual revenue that Henry received because no complete statement was ever drawn up at the time. What we can be certain about is that Francis Bacon's statement of 1622 that Henry collected treasure amounting to nearly £2 million is grossly exaggerated. By the end of the reign Henry's annual revenue was about £113,000, which was a measure of his success in financial affairs. On the other hand, while it is acknowledged that royal financial administration was probably at its most efficient under Henry, recent research by Professor J.R. Lander suggests that 'the net gain was no more than to restore crown income in real terms to what it had been in the late fourteenth and early fifteenth centuries'.

It must be remembered that, in comparison to its European neighbours, the English crown was relatively poor. The King of France, for example, received about £800,000 a year. Nevertheless, Henry had gone further than his Yorkist predecessors: he had not only arrested the decline in royal revenues but also restored the solvency of the crown and, by meticulous attention to detail, inspired a new impetus and greater efficiency into the old financial institutions. Finally, by increasing the annual revenue, his income was nearly 20 times greater than that of his wealthiest noble. Henry had restored to the crown its prestige and given it far greater freedom of action in its policies both at home and abroad.

Study Guide: AS Questions

In the style of AQA

Study the following source material and then answer the questions that follow on page 110.

Source A

Adapted from: Edmund Dudley's petition to Henry VIII while awaiting trial, 1509.

It was the King's pleasure to have many bound to him by great sums of money, some by recognisances, and some by obligation without any conditions but a simple bond payable (to him) at a certain day.

Source B

Adapted from: a description of Henry VII by Polydore Vergil, a papal tax collector, who was well connected at the royal court, 1513.

After 1502 he began to treat his people with more harshness and severity than had been his custom, in order to ensure that they remained more thoroughly and entirely in obedience to him. The people themselves had another explanation for his action, for they felt they were suffering not on account of their own sins, but on account of the greed of the monarch.

Source C

Adapted from: Colin Pendrill, The Wars of the Roses and Henry VII: England 1459–c.1513, *2004.*

Although Henry undoubtedly increased royal income during his reign, the scale of his financial achievement should not be exaggerated. Henry VII did not discover or set up any new sources of revenue for the Crown, but he exploited existing revenues in a more determined and systematic way than his predecessors had. The truth is that throughout his reign Henry raised money and spent money on a scale not seen before. He had to spend a lot of money to defeat his enemies, Simnel in 1487 and Warbeck. At the same time, Henry also spent vast sums on diplomacy. It is entirely predictable that Henry would want to use his new-found wealth to persuade foreign leaders and diplomats that he was here to stay.

(a) Use Source A and your own knowledge
Explain briefly the meaning of 'recognisances' in the context of government under Henry VII. (3 marks)

(b) Use Source B and your own knowledge
Explain how useful Source B is as evidence of Henry VII's treatment of his subjects in the last ten years of his reign. (7 marks)

(c) Use Sources A, B and C and your own knowledge
'Strong finances were the major reason why Henry VII was able to keep his throne'. Explain why you agree or disagree with this opinion. (15 marks)

Source: adapted from AQA, 2002

Exam tips

The cross-references are intended to take you straight to the material that will help you to answer the questions.

1. In question **(a)** you should provide an explanation of recognisances, linked to the context, for example:

   - The acknowledgement of a debt to the crown.
   - The use of recognisances to bind members of the nobility and important officials to the king to ensure they remained loyal and did not rebel (pages 105–6).

2. In question **(b)** you have to understand what is being said in the source and who is saying it in order to evaluate its usefulness. You must consider its strengths and weaknesses, for example it was written:

   - by someone who was well placed to comment on Henry's policies especially in regard to the nobility (pages 44–59).
   - not long after Henry's death so it might not be accurate.

   Support your answer with some examples of Henry's rule, e.g. his use of the Council Learned in the Law and the activities of Empson and Dudley (pages 74–5).

3. In question **(c)** evaluate the extent to which strong finances alone were responsible for Henry keeping his throne, for example:

   - Try to make effective use of the sources together with your own knowledge in order to provide a balanced answer.
   - Provide a range of reasons in addition to strong finances, e.g. control of the nobility, concern with law and order, his use of such institutions as the Council Learned and employment of loyal and efficient officials.

   You should draw on the information contained in the sources together with some appreciation of the reliability of those responsible for expressing their opinions. For example:

   - Differentiate between the largely subjective comments of contemporaries in A and B and the more objective opinion expressed by the historian in C. You are encouraged to reach a substantiated conclusion.

In the style of Edexcel

Study Sources 1–5 below and answer questions (a)–(e) that follow on page 113.

Source 1

From: Polydore Vergil, Anglica Historia, *written in 1513.*

The King wished to keep all Englishmen obedient through fear, and he considered that whenever they gave him offence they were motivated by their great wealth … All of his subjects who were men of substance when found guilty of whatever fault he harshly fined in order by a penalty which especially deprives of their fortunes not only the men themselves but even their descendants, to make the population less well able to undertake any upheaval and to discourage at the same time all offences.

Source 2

From: part of a letter written in 1496, from the Milanese ambassador to his government in Milan.

Everything goes well with the king, especially as he has an immense fortune in his treasury. All the nobles of the realm know the royal wisdom, and … bear him in extraordinary affection. No man of any important rank joins the king's enemies.

Source 3

From: The Great Chronicle of London *recording the City's benevolence of 1491.*

The King … sent for the Mayor [of London] and so handled him, that he caused him to grant towards … his grace … £200. By precedent whereof all the aldermen were fain [encouraged] to do the same … This benevolence was so chargeable unto the City that the whole sum thereof extended unto £9682 17s. 4d. By reason whereof it was named later malevolence for benevolence.

Source 4

From: an illustration drawn in the early years of Henry VIII's reign showing 'Henry VII's tax collectors greedily and eagerly counting out the month's takings'.

Source 5

From: John McGurk, The Tudor Monarchies 1485–1603, *published in 1999.*

Henry may very well have kept the trust and faith of his parliaments by not asking them to grant taxes too often, but he made up for this by fully exploiting all traditional sources of the royal revenue. Dudley became a tireless tax collector and, while so doing, feathered his own nest. Henry VII did not feel secure unless he was rich. A full treasury helps to explain why he was so successful in quelling the rebellions against him; and it took him 15 years before he could feel safe from rival claimants.

(a) **Study Source 1**

What can you learn from Source 1 about Henry's reputation as a ruler? (6 marks)

(b) **Use your own knowledge**

Use your own knowledge to explain the importance of 'attainders'. (10 marks)

(c) **Study Sources 1 and 2**

How far do Sources 1 and 2 support Henry's reputation for greed? (10 marks)

(d) **Study Sources 2 and 4**

How useful are these two sources to an historian studying the importance of finance to the stability of the monarchy in the reign of Henry VII? (10 marks)

(e) **Study Sources 3 and 5 and use your own knowledge**

Do you agree with the view that Henry VII obtained internal security for his realm mainly through his financial policy? Explain your answer, using the two sources and your own knowledge. (24 marks)

Source: adapted from Edexcel, 2001

Exam tips

The cross-references are intended to take you straight to the material that will help you answer the questions.

1. The answer to question **(a)** is to be found entirely within Source 1. You have to show that you have understood the content of the source. You do not have to use your own knowledge but you must infer from the evidence contained in the source. Keep your answer to the point. For example:

    - Henry's reputation as a ruler has largely rested on his assumed financial skill.
    - Henry was ruthless in the pursuit and punishment of his enemies.

2. In question **(b)** you must use your own knowledge to explain the reference to 'attainders'. You should focus your answer on explaining what an attainder was, how it worked and why it was used (page 103).

3. In question **(c)** you have to understand what is being said in Sources 1 and 2. Use your knowledge to explain the link between the references to finance in the sources and what you know about Henry's financial policies and his reputation for greed. Evaluate the extent to which the sources support (or not) the statement in the question (pages 107–8).

4. In question **(d)** you have to focus on the key word 'useful' and suggest ways in which an historian might find Sources 2 and 4 useful in studying the importance of finance to the stability of the monarchy. Remember to consider the captions and attributions – what were the motives of those who either wrote or commissioned the sources? Can they be trusted by the historian? For example:

    - Source 2 suggests that financial reward was a vital factor in maintaining the support of the nobility.
    - Source 4 suggests that the methods of revenue collecting and accounting were efficient.
    - However, you might argue that the pressure to maintain a regular income by whatever means possible could easily affect the stability of the monarchy. Certainly Source 4 was drawn with a view to being critical of Henry VII's financial policy.

5. Question **(e)** carries the greatest number of marks, so deserves the greatest amount of time devoted to it.

    - You have to recall your own knowledge in order to discuss the means by which Henry secured the dynasty.
    - You must assess the contribution the king's financial polices made to securing the dynasty by reference to the sources, the contents of which are there to help you. (You must resist the temptation to copy the source content but specific quotation is permissible if it is used to support a point you are trying to make.)
    - You must also show how his other policies – in government, in foreign affairs and in respect of the nobility – also contributed to securing the dynasty (pages 27–8).
    - You should round off your answer by offering an opinion in respect of how far you agree or disagree with the question.

In the style of OCR

(a) Why, and with what success, did Henry VII strengthen the royal finances? (45 marks)

(b) How far do you agree that Henry VII's financial policies were the most important reason for the stability of his rule? (45 marks)

Source: OCR, 2000

Exam tips

The cross-references are intended to take you straight to the material that will help you to answer the questions.

1. In question **(a)** you should explain why the royal finances needed strengthening and why sound finances were important to Henry and evaluate his success in strengthening the royal finances. Two-thirds of your answer should concentrate on evaluating the success of Henry's financial policies, for example:

   • The royal accounting system and revenue collection was still inefficient in spite of the improvements made under Edward IV and Richard III.
   • Sound finances would enable him to be independent and strong.
   • He needed to repay the debts that had been incurred in his bid for the throne.
   • He needed money to reward loyalty and to defeat any rival claimants to the throne (pages 94–5 and 107–8).

   You need also to evaluate Henry's success in strengthening the finances, for example:

   • The king's financial methods became more efficient which resulted in a corresponding rise in revenue. Henry's success in finance is often hailed to be among his greatest achievements.
   • On the other hand, his methods were too rigorous and his determination to collect all available sources of revenue led to resentment and uprisings.

2. In question **(b)** you should adopt an analytical approach by first evaluating the contribution Henry's financial policies made to the stability of his rule before discussing and evaluating the contribution of his other policies. You must resist the temptation to respond in a narrative way, i.e. by listing and describing the key features of his financial and other policies. For example:

   • Show the ways in which Henry used finance to his advantage in order to consolidate the dynasty, bolster his security and achieve stability in his rule (pages 107–8).
   • However, you must also show how his other policies – in government, in foreign affairs and in respect of the nobility – also contributed to the stability of his rule (pages 161–7).
   • You should round off your answer by offering an opinion in respect of how far you agree or disagree with the question.

6

Stabilising the Economy: Economic Policy and Change

POINTS TO CONSIDER
Henry's primary aim was to stabilise the economy in order to derive financial advantage from the increase in trade and taxation. The problem over enclosures threatened this stability, which is why Henry tried to do something about it. In order to stimulate the economy Henry encouraged industry, particularly the cloth trade, and voyages of exploration. These are examined as five themes:

- Rural society and enclosure
- Urban society and the growth in the merchant class
- Industry
- Trade
- Exploration

Key dates

1485–6	Navigation Acts passed
1489	First acts passed against enclosure
1496	Trade agreement, known as the *Magnus Intercursus*, was signed
1497	John Cabot sailed for America and claimed Newfoundland for England
1506	Commercial treaty, nicknamed the *Malus Intercursus*, was signed

1 | Rural Society and Enclosure

In the late middle ages the economy of England was largely agricultural, with 95 per cent of the population living off the land. The **Black Death** of the mid-fourteenth century had reduced the population by about a third. Further outbreaks of plague, **high infant mortality**, and the ravages of the **Hundred Years War** and the Wars of the Roses had continued the decline: so the population of England, which had been about six million in 1300, was reduced to about two million by 1450. However, by the 1480s numbers were slowly increasing, although they still fluctuated due to periodic bad harvests and outbreaks of plague.

Key question
How and why did the structure of society change?

Black Death
The plague that spread across the British Isles between 1347 and 1351 killing up to half the population.

Key term

High infant mortality
Phrase used to describe the high percentage of deaths suffered by children under the age of five.

Hundred Years War
Term applied by historians to describe the state of war that existed between England and France between 1338 and 1453.

Serfdom
A medieval social and economic system whereby peasants are tied to the land on which they live and work.

Lords spiritual and temporal
Terms used to describe high-ranking churchmen like bishops (lords spiritual) and the nobility like earls and dukes.

Master craftsmen
Skilled workers at the top of their trade.

Paupers and vagrants
The very poor who had no homes and were left to wander from place to place to beg.

Historians agree that events of the late fourteenth and fifteenth centuries fundamentally changed the social structure of England. In the middle ages society was seen in terms of a pyramid of status, in rank, wealth and occupation.

This pyramidal structure was firmly held together by the feudal system, which had been established as far back as the Norman Conquest. Most peasants were serfs who were legally bound to their feudal lords and depended on them for their survival. They had no hope of gaining their freedom.

However this situation was beginning to change by the late fifteenth century. The impact of the Black Death and the subsequent drop in the population led to the relative economic decline of the landowners because many of them had perished in the epidemic and those that were left were forced to pay for the work done on their estates. Consequently, some were forced to lease or sell part of their estates, which created a market in land, making it available to a wider cross-section of society.

This led to an expansion in the size of the élites and to their being less exclusive. They became divided into two parts:

- the nobles, whose rank placed them just below the king
- a new social category, the gentry, the lesser élite group.

The economic crisis also had a profound effect on the peasants at the bottom of the social hierarchy. The decline in the economic power of the landowners began the breakdown of the feudal system. By the beginning of the sixteenth century **serfdom** was almost non-existent, and the peasants were free to move around the country as they liked.

Some peasants took advantage of the availability of land and became commercial farmers, owning a small farm. These better-off peasants were known as yeomen. Some retained their small-holdings and supplemented their incomes by working part-time on the commercial farms. Others took advantage of the increased wage levels created by the reduction in the labour force to work for wages. It was this element of choice for the lower orders, created by greater geographical mobility and fewer people, that was the most significant change in society in the fifteenth century.

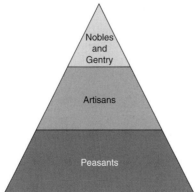

- At the top of this hierarchy were the élite groups: the **lords spiritual and temporal** knights, esquires and gentlemen.

- Next were those distinguished by their occupations: the clergy, lawyers, merchants and **master craftsmen**.

- Finally came the lowest and the largest group – those with neither wealth nor status: labourers, ordinary soldiers, **paupers and vagrants**.

Figure 6.1: Pyramid of status

Enclosure

During the middle ages, land was farmed by the open-field system in many areas. Surrounding each village there were three open fields that were divided into strips and shared out amongst the villagers. A system of rotation was followed so that the soil did not become exhausted. There was also a stretch of common land where the villagers grazed their animals. By the late fifteenth century this practice was being challenged in many areas by enclosure. Enclosure was the fencing-off of land and the abolition of all common rights over it, so that it then became solely the responsibility of its individual owner, who could use it in whatever way he wished. In the open-field system, however, decisions about the way in which the land would be used had been made collectively by all those who farmed it.

Key question
What was enclosure and why was it such a serious problem?

Advantages of enclosure
- The advantages of enclosure were particularly marked in districts where the land was more suited to sheep farming than to the growing of arable crops.
- The enclosers could divide their land into properly fenced off fields, which was not possible with the open-field system.
- They could then, for instance, practise **selective breeding** of animals, or develop their own techniques without being held back by their less adventurous neighbours.
- This was particularly true of the Midlands where farmers were still benefiting from changing from **arable** to **pasture farming**. The problems resulting from enclosure would also be most apparent in this area.

Key terms

Selective breeding Ensuring that only the most healthy animals were allowed to breed to strengthen the blood-line.

Arable farming Crop growing.

Pasture farming Animal rearing.

Disadvantages of enclosure

Enclosure also brought disadvantages to some sections of the community. It could lead to the eviction of families who could not prove that they had a legal right to part of the land which was to be enclosed, or to the loss of the right to use common land for grazing and for the collection of fire wood. John Hales, an enclosure commissioner in the reign of Edward VI, distinguished clearly between fair and unfair enclosure in this statement to jurors charged with investigating the problem in 1548:

> Where a man doth enclose and hedge in his own proper ground, where no man hath commons ... such enclosure is very beneficial to the commonwealth. But when any man hath taken away and enclosed any other men's commons, or hath pulled down houses and converted the lands from tillage to pasture; this is most evilly done.

Enclosure was a very contentious issue in the late fifteenth and early sixteenth centuries and there were many petitions to the king and to parliament against it. However, historians now think that enclosure was not as serious an issue as was once thought, although contemporaries believed it was.

- First, it had been practised for centuries before Henry's reign, so was not a new problem.
- Second, during the fifteenth century, when the population was low and the workforce small, many landlords had turned to pasture farming as the only viable way of using their land, as they could not recruit enough labour to grow arable crops on it.
- Third, in the Midlands, where the problem was most concentrated, less than three per cent of the region was enclosed.
- Fourth, most of the enclosure was done with the consent of both the lord and the tenant.

Therefore, the much complained of injustices of enclosure must be kept in proportion. In certain cases it did lead to eviction, the depopulation of villages and occasionally **vagabondage**, but the extent of this has been exaggerated. Enforced enclosure was still quite rare and most of the worst cases of it had already occurred when Henry came to the throne. The **engrossing** of farms was a practice that was often associated with enclosure and was not infrequently confused with it, even by contemporaries. This undoubtedly had a detrimental effect on rural society, in that it often resulted in people being evicted and made homeless.

Acts against enclosure

Of course, the governments of the time did not have the benefit of historical research at their disposal and they failed to distinguish between the problems caused by enclosure and those that resulted from engrossing. Henry's parliament passed the first legislation against enclosure in 1489, although its terms were motivated by a desire to protect the interests of the crown rather than those of the people adversely affected by the changes. It was specifically aimed at the Isle of Wight on the grounds that the depopulation of the island was a threat to the defence of the realm.

Later in the same year another, more general, act was passed which was the forerunner of legislation in succeeding reigns. Although the word enclosure was not used in the act, its preface did criticise the conversion of arable to pasture, the decay of villages, churches and defences, and unemployment, which it linked to the breakdown of law and order. In an attempt to prevent depopulation, the act forbade the destruction of houses attached to 20 or more acres of land.

However, this was never successfully implemented because its enforcement was left to the landlords, who were the very people to benefit from the actions the legislation was designed to prevent. Although it displayed confusion about the practice of enclosure, the act did at least reveal that Henry's government was beginning to accept some responsibility for solving social problems, even if it misunderstood their causes.

Key terms

Vagabondage
To be landless and unemployed.

Engrossing
Where two or more farms combined to make a more economic unit.

Key date

To protect the crown's interests, parliament passed the first of a series of Acts to deal with enclosure: 1489

2 | Urban Society: Towns and Merchants

Towns

In the late middle ages about five per cent of the population lived in towns. The Black Death had reduced the population of most towns by about a third and, in some cases, had wiped out entire communities. Further outbreaks of plague and the ravages of foreign and civil war had continued the decline.

The population of England's towns, which had been about 300,000 in 1300, was reduced to about 100,000 by 1450. However, by the 1490s numbers were slowly increasing and there were about 700 towns in England, all small except London, which numbered 50,000 people. The other larger provincial towns together made up only two per cent of the population, and the most important of these, such as Bristol or Norwich, did not exceed 10,000 people, while most had under 1000.

The town was the centre of trade in a largely rural environment. It was an agricultural centre, a place which turned the raw material of the countryside into goods for sale. It was also a place of exchange, in ideas as well as goods, which had the privilege of holding markets and fairs. The life, trade and economy of the town were controlled by its members, the burgesses. The majority of burgesses were artisans or craftsmen who lived and traded in the town, and became privileged members of its community.

Key question
What were towns like at this time?

Guilds and burgesses

The craftsmen represented every kind of trade that might be found in a town: for example, in the town records of Exeter we read of bakers, barbers, butchers, card-makers, carpenters, drapers, dyers, haberdashers, leather-tanners, masons, painters, saddlers, shearmen, smiths, tailors, tilers and weavers. Each trade or occupation formed itself into a guild to promote and protect its interest. The guild also fixed hours of work, wages and, more importantly, prices. By 1500 London had 66 guilds while York had 47. The wealthier members of these guilds tended to become leading burgesses who came to dominate the government of the town.

During the fifteenth century some guilds became wealthier and more influential than others and the more powerful of them received charters from the king. Two of the most important were the **Merchant Taylors** and **Merchant Staplers**, but they were swallowed up by the growth of the Merchant Adventurers. The Merchant Adventurers were not tied to any one trade or guild but represented a wide cross-section of the merchant community in England's ports and towns.

Key question
What part did the guilds and burgesses play in the economic life of a town?

Key terms

Merchant Taylors
Guild or union of merchants concerned with the cloth trade.

Merchant Staplers
Guild or union of merchants concerned with the export of raw wool.

The Merchant Adventurers

During the fifteenth century the merchants in the more important towns of England came together to organise themselves into trading companies. Collectively they became known as Merchant Adventurers. In port towns like Bristol,

Key question
Why did the Merchant Adventurers become so powerful?

industrial towns like Newcastle and agricultural towns like Norwich, the Merchant Adventurers dominated the local economy and controlled trade. However, the most important trading companies were to be found in London and, when they came together, they formed the most powerful group within the Merchant Adventurers. London merchants steadily took control of the merchant companies of other ports (except Bristol which retained its independence) and towns so that by 1500 the headquarters of the Merchant Adventurers was firmly based in the kingdom's capital. In 1505 Henry VII granted the Merchant Adventurers a charter whereby they were to appoint a governor with 24 assistants to run the organisation.

The role of the merchants was important because they encouraged and promoted trade, which contributed to the nation's finances. The growth in trade and foreign imports resulted in increased customs duties. This, in turn, encouraged successive kings of England to patronise them. In times of peace Henry was even prepared to rent the seven ships of his navy to merchants. In return for his patronage, Henry expected the merchants to support him by providing loans to help finance his

A gauger at work. The gauger was an early type of weights and measures inspector. Henry introduced a new standard of weights and measures – why do you think he did this?

government. For example, he borrowed sums in excess of £10,000 from the Merchant Staplers of Calais, the only part of France still ruled by England, and from the Merchant Adventurers of London. The loans were usually short term and were repaid in full. The king also expected the merchants to support his foreign policy even if it meant them losing trade or having to break contracts with foreign companies. The merchants had to accept that Henry's economic measures often served non-economic ends: his primary aim was peace and security.

3 | Industry

The wool and cloth industry

Key question
Why was the cloth industry so important to the nation's economy?

The production of cloth made from wool had become the country's major industry by the fifteenth century, accounting for about 90 per cent of English exports. The manufacture of woollen cloth to some extent healed the wound opened by the change of arable to pasture farming, for which the cloth trade was chiefly responsible. Initially English wool had been exported raw. It was of the highest quality and was consequently in great demand in European markets. English kings were quick to realise the advantages of this and levied heavy duties on its export.

By the beginning of Henry's reign the export of raw wool had halved and was being overtaken by that of woollen cloth. Because of the success of the cloth industry it is often overlooked that England was technically backward by continental standards in the manufacture of commodities such as linen, silk, leather and glass. Apart from woollen cloth, England had virtually no manufactured goods to export and the variety of goods imported shows how dependent the country was on industry abroad. As with many industrial jobs at the time, those in the English woollen industry were frequently only part-time occupations shared with agricultural work. For this reason, it is difficult to identify a separate industrial section of society.

Employment in the cloth industry

The dramatic increase in the export of cloth at the expense of wool made very little difference to England's agriculture, but it did have a significant impact on trade and employment. The expansion of the cloth industry was greatly helped by the upward trend in the population, creating a larger pool of available labour. Many of the processes involved in the cloth industry were well suited to the domestic environment and took place in the home: children carded (untangled the fibres) the wool, women span it and men wove the fabric and sometimes finished it off ready for the next stage of the process. It only left the home for fulling (a cleaning process by beating and scouring) and dyeing.

The wool was distributed to the outworkers by a clothier who organised and financed the operation. This led to the development of an economic and social hierarchy within the woollen industry. At one end was the family, spinning and weaving and dependent on the clothier for their raw material and livelihood, and at the other was the rich wool merchant, organising all the stages from the distribution of the raw wool to its sale as lengths of cloth in London.

The three main districts in which woollen cloth was manufactured were the West Riding of Yorkshire, East Anglia and the West Country. In some areas, like Wiltshire, families were wholly dependent on the cloth trade for their livelihoods. Small market towns, such as Lavenham in Suffolk and Totnes in Devon, prospered from the proceeds of the trade. Such communities as these farmed on a small scale as well, so there was less fear of unemployment than in areas that were totally dependent on agriculture.

However, there was always the danger of war on the continent, bad harvests, or plague disrupting trade. This could result in a drop in demand, less money to spend, and consequently people temporarily out of work. Although some could survive these slumps by turning to work on the land, for the totally urban workers there was no alternative but to resort to begging until trade picked up again. Unemployment was a relatively new experience in the sixteenth century, and the fact that Henry's government did not know how to set about lessening the hardship that it caused is hardly surprising.

The linen industry

Key question
How important was the linen industry?

The making of woollen cloth continued to dominate the English textile industry until well into the eighteenth century, but there were already the beginnings of the production of a variety of other types of fabric in various parts of the country. In Lancashire there was the beginning of a linen industry making use of local flax; this supplemented its reliance on the import of Irish yarn to maintain its output of coarse woollens on which its people depended for work as well as for clothes. Linen making was also carried out in other parts of the country but on a smaller scale. Hand-knitting, primarily for the production of stockings which were worn by men as well as by women, provided extra income for the poorer peasants in the Lake District and the Cotswolds.

The metal industries

Key question
How important were the metal and coal industries?

There were other non-agrarian industries in England at this time. Tin and lead mining both satisfied the home market and were profitable exports. The main areas of lead mining were the Pennines, north and central Wales and the Mendips; Devon and particularly Cornwall were famous for their tin mining, and their high-quality products dominated European markets by the sixteenth century. There was the beginning of a brass-making industry based on the mining of copper in Cumberland and zinc ore in the Mendips and metallurgical skills brought from Germany. By the beginning of the sixteenth century such exchange of technological expertise with Europe was not unusual. There is further evidence of it in the introduction of charcoal-fuelled blast furnaces for smelting which led to the production of cast-iron in Sussex and Kent, the iron-ore areas.

The coal industry

Coal had been mined since the thirteenth century and was exported from the Durham and Northumberland fields in particular. By Henry's reign there is evidence that the output of coal was beginning to accelerate because in areas where timber was scarce it was cheaper to transport coal by water than to bring in wood from other areas. Coal was gradually becoming an important source of fuel for the poor, especially in London.

Conclusion

Despite these innovations, England was still industrially backward by continental standards. Apart from the manufacture of woollen cloth, industry was on a very small scale. For the most part it provided only **casual labour** for a fraction of the population – work that fluctuated with rises and falls in demand and was at the mercy of the seasons and natural disasters such as flooding. In 1500 England could not be described as an industrial country; her industries (except cloth) employed only small numbers of labourers with an even smaller core of skilled men – hardly the beginnings of a capitalistic society!

4 | Trade

While building up a fortune for himself, Henry did not neglect the prosperity of his subjects. His 'thrifty mind could not endure to see trade sick' wrote Bacon (1622), and he worked hard to re-establish English commerce which had declined and passed into the hands of foreigners during the upheavals of government in the recent civil wars. The king recognised the importance of flourishing trade to a healthy economy, which in turn would strengthen the Tudors' hold on the throne. If trade was to expand then the necessary ships had to be available to carry goods. The importance that Henry attached to this is evident because it was one of the earliest tasks he tackled.

Navigation Acts

When Henry came to the throne England's shipping was inferior to its European counterparts. Most of the country's trade was carried in foreign ships, particularly those of the **Hanseatic League**. Henry intended to break Hanseatic control of English trade with northern Europe, and that of other foreign merchants too.

By the Navigation Acts of 1485–6 he attempted to limit the foreign grip on English trade. The acts forbade Englishmen to load their goods on foreign ships when English ones were available, and reserved the lucrative trade with Bordeaux in France exclusively for the English. So, from 1486, wines from Gascony were to be imported only in English ships with crews made up of no less than 50 per cent of the king's subjects. A further act in 1489 stipulated that English merchants should only import goods in foreign ships if no English ones were available.

The subsequent reaction from the Hanse and similar swift retaliation from Spain is evidence that it had the desired effect.

The navy

Key question
How and why did England develop a navy?

Kings of England no more kept a navy than a regular army, because it would have been just as expensive to maintain. However, in time of war, merchant vessels could be transformed into fighting ships, so there was an important link between trade and defence. Henry fully appreciated this fact and encouraged wealthy merchants to build vessels of not less than 80 tonnes, which could be transformed into effective fighting ships when necessary. Yet Henry's reign is not famous for its naval record, unlike Henry VIII's or Elizabeth I's. He did not bequeath his son a significant number of ships as some of his predecessors had done: Henry V left 34 in 1422, Edward IV left 15 in 1483 but Henry VII left only nine ships.

However, Henry did at least establish the basis of a proper navy, small though it was. Nevertheless, what Henry VII's navy lacked in numbers, it made up for in quality. His ships were bigger, better equipped and more efficiently administered than those of previous periods. The 600-tonne *Regent*, which carried 225 cast-iron guns weighing 250 pounds (113 kg) each, was a force to be reckoned with and the forerunner of more effective warships. The king also constructed the navy's first fortified naval base at Portsmouth. Henry was now more prepared to defend his island kingdom at sea, and had laid the foundations of naval defence on which his son and granddaughter were so successfully to build.

The cloth trade

Key question
How important was the cloth trade and how did it affect foreign policy?

Early in Henry's reign, in 1489, an act was passed which forbade foreign buyers from purchasing wool until English merchants had bought all they wanted. This was a deliberate move to show the new king's recognition of this flourishing industry. The same act also made it illegal for foreigners to buy wool for manufacture into cloth outside England. This was intended to restrict the export of raw wool and by the end of Henry's reign it was 30 per cent lower than it had been in 1485. This was also partly due to heavy taxes on the export of raw wool and the increasing demands of the native cloth industry. Meanwhile the export of woollen cloth flourished and 60 per cent more cloth was being exported in 1509 than had been at the beginning of the reign.

Antwerp was the major recipient of English cloth. However, the activities of the pretenders and the changing nature of foreign policy meant that Henry was sometimes forced to find other markets. This was not particularly difficult as English cloth was in considerable demand and buyers would go wherever it was sold. In 1493, when Perkin Warbeck was enjoying the support of Margaret of Burgundy, Henry issued a **trade embargo** against the Netherlands and ordered the Merchant Adventurers, who exported most English cloth, to move to Calais. The ruler of the Netherlands responded with a counter-embargo on English trade.

Key term

Trade embargo
A country's refusal to trade with another.

Magnus Intercursus

This embargo benefited no-one and so, with the failure of Warbeck and the need of Philip of Burgundy to acquire English support against France (see page 150), the *Magnus Intercursus* was signed in 1496. This treaty stated that English merchants would be allowed to sell their goods wholesale anywhere in Philip, the Duke of Burgundy's dominions, except Flanders, without paying any tolls or customs. They would also receive impartial justice in the local courts.

This could have provided a foundation upon which healthy commercial relations could be built as it was fair to both sides, but the Merchant Adventurers continued to come into frequent conflict with the government of the Netherlands. There were continued disputes as Philip first tried unsuccessfully to impose a new import duty on English traders, and then to confine them to Antwerp. Nor did Henry ease the situation by attempting to negotiate the surrender of the Earl of Suffolk (see pages 40–1).

Malus Intercursus

Then in 1506 fate seemed to play into Henry's hands when Philip, on route to Spain, was forced by fierce storms to seek refuge in an English port. As Henry's guest, Philip was persuaded to agree to a new trading agreement, the *Malus Intercursus*, as Bacon nicknamed it because it was so one-sided. According to the terms of the commercial treaty between Henry VII and Philip of Burgundy, it was agreed that:

- Trade between England and the Low Countries would be free.
- English merchants were to be allowed to anchor and remain at anchor in Philip's harbours and to transport their goods without any charge unless they were sold or unloaded.
- Philip's subjects were to pay the customary English duties as defined by the treaty of 1496.
- Philip and his heirs were not to exclude English cloth from their dominions nor prohibit their use nor impose any duties upon their sale.

In fact, the treaty was never a realistic basis on which satisfactory commercial relations could be carried out. It was too biased towards the English. Philip died soon afterwards, so it was never put into practice.

In 1507 the *Magnus Intercursus* once more became the basis on which trading was practised between England and Burgundy. Henry had used trade as a negotiating weapon to protect his crown: his policy towards trade with the Netherlands had shown that the security of his throne was his priority. He had encouraged and stimulated the cloth trade across the Channel and negotiated the basis of good commercial relations for the future, but he had been prepared to abandon this at any time that it appeared to run contrary to his dynastic interests.

Henry realised that the expansion of overseas trade would boost England's economy and wealth. He also realised how easily trade and dynastic issues could become interwoven and influence

Key dates

Trade agreement between England and Burgundy, known as the *Magnus Intercursus*, was signed: 1496

Commercial treaty between England and Burgundy, nicknamed the *Malus Intercursus* by Francis Bacon, was signed: 1506

the decisions he made. However, it is difficult to identify any consistency in his commercial policy. It was primarily opportunist, and the desire to secure trading advantages always took second place to the need to guarantee the peace and security of the realm.

Trade with France

Key question
How important was the trade with France?

Henry was keen to extend English trade abroad, particularly as the activities of the pretenders had shown how vulnerable was his dependence on Antwerp. So in 1486 Henry began negotiating a new commercial agreement which removed the restrictions on Franco-English trade. However, the dispute over Brittany jeopardised this (see pages 142–4) and resulted in higher duties being charged on English goods imported into France. These were modified under the Treaty of Étaples in 1492 (see pages 144–5), but it was not until 1497 that good relations were finally restored by the removal of these impositions. For the rest of Henry's reign English merchants enjoyed unrestricted trade with the French.

Italy and the Mediterranean trade

Key question
What was the nature of England's trade with Italy and the Mediterranean?

Key terms

Tariff
Tax on imported goods.

Staple
Company concerned with the export of raw wool.

Henry was also keen to develop English trade in the Mediterranean, particularly with Florence. This was to counter the powerful influence of the Venetians, who controlled the trade in luxury goods from the east and with whom England had a long-standing **tariff** war over wines from the Levant. English merchants wished to take an active part in Mediterranean trade and had been prevented from doing so in the past by the Venetians. Their galleys carried most of the luxury goods and wines to northern Europe, and this trading domination was reflected in their high prices.

Henry was determined to challenge this. After he had encouraged a few English ships to sail to the Levant and to return with cargoes of malmsey (a strong, sweet wine) in 1488, the Venetians imposed a huge duty against the English. Henry retaliated with a duty on Venetian-borne malmsey and then approached Venice's arch-rival, Florence. A treaty of 1490 with Florence provided for the establishment of an English **staple**, the only Italian outlet for English wool, at Pisa, the port of the nearby city of Florence and restricted England's wool sales to Venice. The Venetians gave in, fearing that their wool supply would fall entirely into the hands of Florence, and they waived the duty on English shipping in the Levant.

Henry's aggressive strategy had won the day. Whether the Venetians would have allowed the English to maintain this lucrative position is doubtful but, fortunately for the king, Venice was distracted by the outbreak of the Italian Wars in 1494 and had no time to waste on a petty commercial squabble with England. So English merchants were able to take advantage of the situation to increase their trade in the Mediterranean.

Trade with Spain and Portugal

The most important commercial *coup* of the reign was the trade agreement he arranged with Spain. The English already had a successful trade link with Spain's neighbour, Portugal, and in 1489 Henry renewed this established treaty. Recently united Spain, with her dominant role in the voyages of exploration to the **New World**, offered exciting possibilities in trade. The Spanish had enjoyed a very favourable position in the reign of Edward IV, which gave them exemption from the duties payable by other foreigners (except the Hanse) on the import of English goods. Henry had confirmed these privileges at the beginning of his reign but had restricted them somewhat by the Navigation Acts.

The Spanish retaliated, forbidding the export of goods from Spain in foreign ships when native ones were available, but the Treaty of Medina del Campo of 1489 ended this restriction. Although it is best remembered for finalising the marriage between Prince Arthur and Catherine of Aragon, the commercial aspects of the treaty were very important. From 1489 both sides were on equal terms, receiving the same rights in each other's country and with duties fixed at an advantageously low rate. In terms of diplomacy the treaty was a high point for Henry, but the Spanish never allowed him to become as involved in trade with the New World as he would have liked.

The Hanseatic League and Baltic trade

Henry was less successful in his commercial activities in the Baltic. The merchants of the Hanseatic League jealously guarded the virtually exclusive privileges they enjoyed in trade with ports around the Baltic Sea. They also vigorously defended their right, which had been granted to them by Edward IV, to be exempt from duties on goods exported from England, although they failed to observe their promise in return to allow English merchants free access to the Hanse ports.

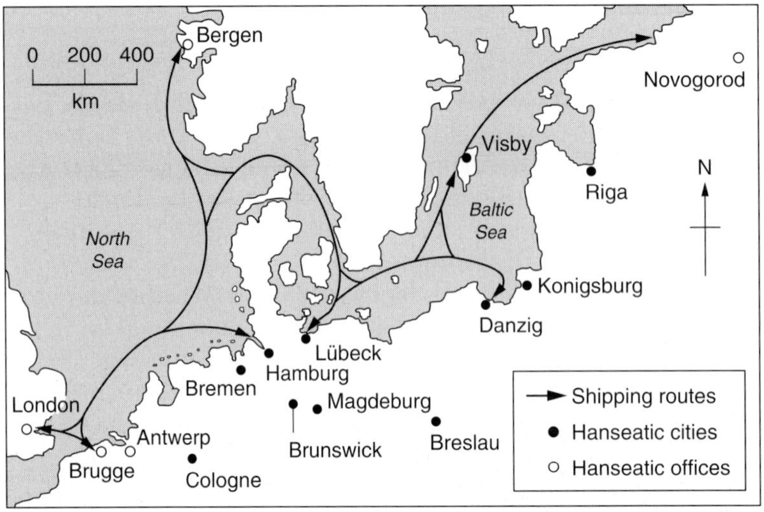

Key question
Why was trade with Spain and Portugal so important?

New World
Term applied to the American continent and associated Caribbean islands recently discovered by Columbus.

Key term

Key question
Why was the Hanseatic League so powerful?

Figure 6.2: The Hanseatic League

Henry had to tread warily in his dealings over this dispute because the Hanse was well placed to cause trouble by supporting pretenders to the English throne. The Navigation Act was the first blow he aimed at them (see pages 124–5), but in fact it did little to reduce their privileges. Then he tried to avoid retaliation by confirming the rights bestowed on them in the previous reign. What Henry wanted was to bypass the Hanse and sell English cloth in northern markets where merchants were eager to exchange it for corn and naval stores.

The tactic he used was to build up resentment among the Hanse merchants in the hope that they would want to take the matter to a conference. This would give him an opportunity to negotiate the ending of the one-sided treaty agreed under Edward IV.

Therefore, an act of parliament was passed forbidding any foreigners, including Hansards, from exporting unfinished cloth to England. A later act stipulated that they were not allowed to take money out of the country. To add further provocation, English merchants who captured Hanse ships went unpunished and German merchants were unable to walk safely in the streets of the capital.

Challenging the Hanse

The king restricted the Hanse's privilege of importing their goods at preferential rates by interpreting the phrase of the treaty to mean only goods produced in their own territories. When the conference that Henry had hoped for finally took place at Antwerp in 1491 an amicable solution could not be reached.

The Hanseatic League's depot in London.

Henry's other method of dealing with the Hanse was similar to that used against Venice – joining with his target's major rival and attempting to out-manoeuvre them. In 1489 a treaty with Denmark brought English merchants into competition with the Hanse for the Scandinavian trade and gave the English the right to fish in Icelandic waters. Another opportunity arose in 1499 when a treaty with Riga on the Baltic coast (modern-day Latvia) seemed to create a considerable dent in the Hanse's Baltic monopoly, but this did not last long as Riga soon returned to the Hanseatic League and the treaty was not renewed. So Henry could only temporarily challenge the influence of the Hanse: it was too powerful a body to be overcome permanently.

A settlement only occurred when Henry gave in completely to the Hanse. An act of 1504 restored the Hanse to the favourable position it had enjoyed under Edward IV. This extraordinary u-turn by the king was certainly not dictated by economic considerations. The only satisfactory explanation is that Henry was deeply concerned with the exploits of the Earl of Suffolk who was at this time winning support on the continent, particularly in northern Europe (see pages 40–1). He must have feared that the Hanse would seek their revenge by supporting this Yorkist rebel. Yet the loss of trading advantage seems out of all proportion to the actual dynastic risks involved.

Henry's achievements

Key question
How successful was Henry's commercial policy?

In assessing the success of Henry's commercial policy it is not possible to reach a simple conclusion. He did undoubtedly increase the outlets for English trade, and he deserves credit for the forward-looking treaty with Spain and the openings he forged with Venice and in Scandinavia. However, his achievements did not, as he had hoped, greatly benefit his financial position. Although the customs revenue rose at the beginning of the reign, this was probably as much a result of the more efficient collection of customs duties as of any expansion of trade. However, English shipping did expand under his patronage and by 1509 English merchants were shipping more cloth abroad than the combined exports of all other merchants.

Nevertheless, English trade, apart from that with the Netherlands, was still on a small scale compared with that of Venice or Spain. As in his dealings with the Hanse and the Netherlands, dynastic considerations were always his first priority, and valuable possibilities were sacrificed on more than one occasion in the interests of the security of his regime. For example, Henry stopped trading with the Netherlands for a time because of its ruler's support for Warbeck. Although Henry had opened doors in the Mediterranean and the Baltic, this was as much as he had achieved. What Henry had done was to begin the development of English trade, but it was left to his successors to build on the very limited start he had made.

5 | Exploration

Key question
What was the nature and extent of Henry's contribution to exploration?

One of the most original of Henry's interests was in the geographical discoveries of the age. He gave financial support to John and Sebastian Cabot, as well as to many less well-known men who participated in the exploration of the New World that was being discovered on the far side of the Atlantic (see Figure 6.3, page 132). If his successors had followed his example, English domination of the North American mainland might have come about much earlier than it did. However, Henry has been criticised for turning down the patronage of **Christopher Columbus** at the very beginning of his reign. In fact, the king himself was particularly intrigued by Columbus' proposals to attempt a trans-Atlantic voyage, but the idea was rejected by the council who thought that the plan badly misjudged the size of the ocean.

Key term

Christopher Columbus
Italian explorer who discovered America for Spain in 1492.

Historians now realise that the decision not to support the venture probably did not rob England of an early lead in the trans-Atlantic race because it is likely that had Columbus set out from this country, rather than from Spain as he did, the winds would only have swept him to the shores of Nova Scotia and not the more inviting islands of the Caribbean. Henry's obvious regret when he learnt of Columbus' successful voyage to the New World with all the lucrative trade that it offered his patron, Spain, is shown when he seized the opportunity to finance John Cabot.

John Cabot

Key date

With the support of Henry, John Cabot sailed for America which he reached claiming Newfoundland for England: 1497

John Cabot was born in Genoa, Italy and was an experienced sailor in the Mediterranean and the east. He arrived in England in 1495 and obtained an audience with the king early the following year. Cabot thought that if he sailed west in a more northerly latitude than Columbus had done, he would shorten the distance to the Far East, which was the goal of all the early westward explorers. Lured by the prospect of the profits to be made from the eastern trade in exotic luxuries and spices, Henry authorised Cabot and his sons to 'sail to all parts, regions and coasts of the eastern, western and northern sea'.

However, Henry's cautious nature did not desert him: he gave them £50 for the voyage but would not commit himself to further support until he had proof of the success of this first venture. Unfortunately, stormy weather rendered the voyage a disaster. In 1497 Cabot set out a second time and, after a journey lasting five weeks, land was sighted. Where on the American mainland this was is still uncertain, but the banners of Henry VII and the Pope were duly planted. It was most likely somewhere on the coast of Newfoundland as Cabot comments in his log that there were more cod in the waters than in Iceland. Cabot himself never returned from this expedition but died on the way home.

Sebastian Cabot

More successful was the voyage of his son, Sebastian, in 1509. With the blessing of Henry, the younger Cabot sailed with two

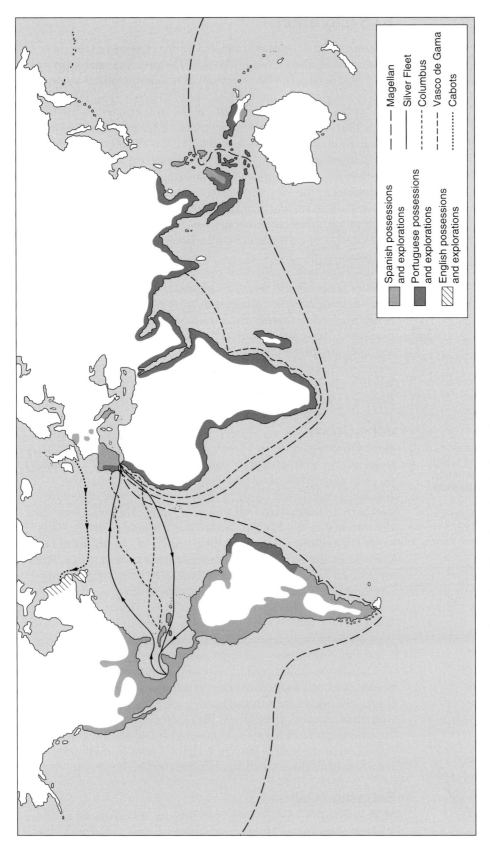

Figure 6.3: Exploration and expansion in the late fifteenth and early sixteenth century

ships to seek a north-west passage around America to Asia. By now it was accepted that America was a continent distinct from Asia, although, of course, it was not yet known that it was impossible for ships to reach Asia by skirting it to the north. Cabot sailed past the most southerly tip of Greenland and across the Davis Strait, finding an opening on its farthest side. He then found himself in open sea. He was convinced that he had rounded America and was in the ocean leading to Cathay (modern-day China). At this point, because of the dangers of drifting ice, he was forced to turn back by his crew. Nevertheless, Cabot believed that he had found the opening to the east by sailing in a north-westerly direction. In fact the channel he had sailed through was the Hudson Strait, and his new ocean was the Hudson Bay.

Henry's reputation as a patron of exploration

Sadly, when Cabot reached England with his exciting news, his former royal patron was dead and the new king had interests other than those of exploration. Henry VII has been described as being only second to Ferdinand and Isabella (see page 146) in patronising the discovery of the New World. If the impetus for these discoveries came from Spain, Henry still deserves credit for the encouragement he gave to those brave enough to face the dangers of the North Atlantic. Numerous expeditions ventured forth because of his offer of large rewards to those who developed commercial links with the New World or the east.

Owing to Henry's patronage, England had more knowledge of North America than any other European country. Unfortunately this advantage was not exploited in the future because of Henry VIII's lack of support for exploration. Mary did renew some interest in this activity but only briefly, and it was really left to Elizabeth to re-establish English interest in maritime activity.

Summary diagram: The English economy 1485–1509

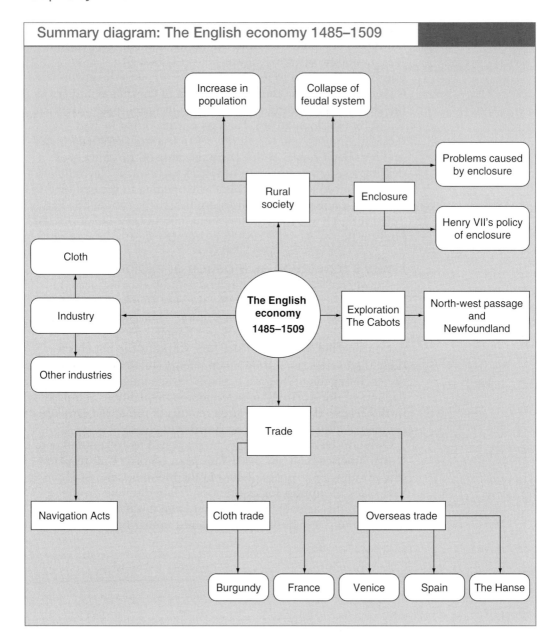

Study Guide: AS Questions

In the style of AQA

Read the following source and then answer the questions that follow.

Adapted from: Roger Lockyer and Dan O'Sullivan, Tudor Britain 1485–1603, *1997.*

The cloth trade was entirely in the hands of the Merchant Adventurers. It was also increasingly focused on London in the reign of Henry VII.

(a) Using the source and your own knowledge, comment on the 'Merchant Adventurers' in the context of the cloth trade during Henry VII's reign. (3 marks)

(b) Explain why the cloth trade was 'increasingly focused on London'. (7 marks)

(c) How important, in relation to other factors, was the export of cloth to Europe in explaining the development of the English economy? (15 marks)

Source: AQA, 2002

Exam tips

The cross-references are intended to take you straight to the material that will help you to answer the questions.

1. In question **(a)** you should provide a developed explanation of the term and its significance in relation to the context and the source, for example:

   - It refers to a London-based merchant company that controlled the cloth trade (pages 122–3).
   - They shipped the cloth for sale in Antwerp and later Calais (page 125).
   - They operated as an exclusive club (pages 120–2).

2. In question **(b)** you need to explain why the cloth trade was centred in London, for example:

   - The city's growing population provided a market (pages 120–2).
   - It was close to the centre of power and government.
   - The Merchant Adventurers received patronage from successive kings including Henry VII (pages 120–2).
   - The monopolistic tendencies of the Merchant Adventurers restricted the export of woollen cloth to London.

3. In question **(c)** you should provide a clear judgement on whether the export of cloth was or was not more important than other factors in the development of the economy, as well as providing a wide range of well-developed examples in support of your arguments. For example, you should try to evaluate the importance of the cloth trade when compared to other industries such as the growing metal trades in the West Midlands and South Yorkshire or the increasingly specialised farming in the south east of England due to the growth of London (pages 122–4).

In the style of OCR

(a) How far was the development of the English economy in the period between 1485 and 1509 due to the influence of King Henry VII? (45 marks)

(b) 'The importance of wool in the English economy has been overestimated.' How far would you agree with this statement? (45 marks)

Exam tips

The cross-references are intended to take you straight to the material that will help you to answer the questions.

1. You must adopt an analytical rather than a narrative approach to answering question **(a)**, for example you must compare and evaluate the reason mentioned (influence of Henry VII) in the question with other equally relevant reasons rather than simply offer a descriptive list of causes.

    - The question is correct to say that Henry's economic policies did contribute to the development of England's economy (e.g. Navigation Acts, trade treaties, royal patronage of merchant organisations), but there were other factors, for example:
        - The growth in population and the more peaceful conditions of the time stimulated the economy (pages 116–19).
        - England could not fail to be affected by the growth in European economies and the resulting increase in trade.
        - Henry's foreign policies frequently hindered trade and economic growth, e.g. the temporary suspension of the wool trade with the Netherlands, because of its ruler's support for Perkin Warbeck, hurt the English economy (page 147).

2. In question **(b)** you should adopt an analytical approach by first evaluating the contribution wool made to the economy before examining the contribution other industries made to the nation's economy, for example:

    - Show the way in which wool and its associated trade in cloth contributed to the economic prosperity of England – in terms of employment, wealth generated by exports, sales at home, taxes to the government (pages 122–30).
    - However, you must also show how other industries (coal, metals) also contributed to the growth of the economy (pages 122–4).
    - You should round off your answer by offering an opinion in respect of how far you agree or disagree with the question.

7 Diplomacy and Alliance: Henry's Foreign Policy

POINTS TO CONSIDER

Henry pursued an active and energetic foreign policy but he steered clear of confrontation and war unless they could not be avoided. His key aims were to be recognised by his fellow monarchs, secure trade and to defeat the pretenders and any other threat to his throne. These are examined as five themes:

- The European situation in 1485
- Developing diplomacy
- Successful diplomacy
- Changing diplomacy
- How successful was Henry?

Key dates

1489	In order to secure allies against France, Henry signed the treaties of Medina del Campo and Redon with Spain and Brittany respectively
1492	Treaty of Étaples restored peaceful relations with France
1495–6	Henry joined the anti-French alliance known as the League of Venice (1495), later re-named the Holy League (1496)
1496	Trade agreement between England and Burgundy, known as *Magnus Intercursus*, ended hostilities between them
1497	Truce of Ayton restored peaceful relations with Scotland
1502	Treaty of Ayton established peace with Scotland
1506	*Malus Intercursus* forced Burgundy to sign commercial treaty favourable to England
1508	Henry formed an anti-Spanish alliance known as the League of Cambrai

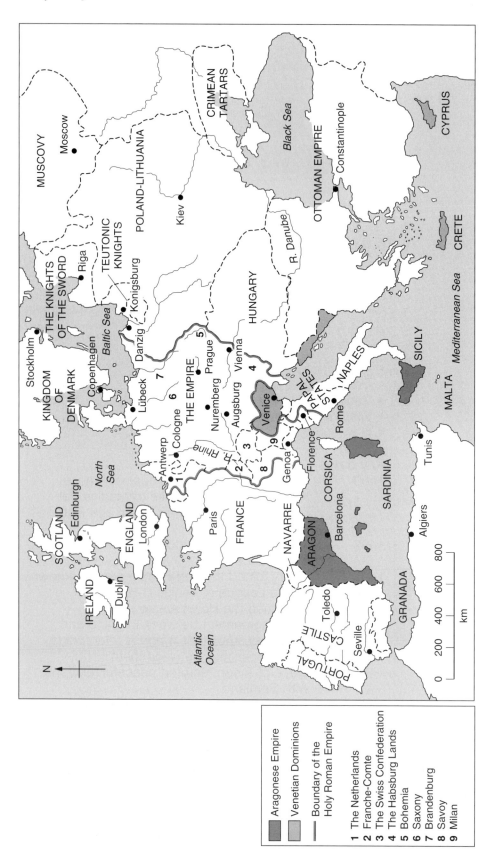

Figure 7.1: A political map of Europe in 1490

Key question
What was Europe like in 1485?

1 | Europe in 1485

Most people prefer to live in peace, and the people who lived during the middle ages were no exception. They believed this was the way of life that God had ordained for man. As God's representative on earth, the king was expected to maintain this ordered existence. On the other hand, if a ruler was challenged in an aggressive manner by a foreign power, then war was acceptable as a form of defence. In such circumstances kings were expected to win great victories for the honour of their subjects.

Obviously, this was a simple view of the relations between states and they were far more complex in reality, particularly by the late fifteenth century. Diplomacy in this period had become more subtle and wide-ranging than before. This was because communication was swifter due to better roads on land and better ships at sea. Decisions were being taken by increasingly powerful and ambitious rulers who knew much more than their predecessors of the world outside their immediate localities because of better maps. This will become clearer as we survey the situation of Europe in 1485 and the factors that influenced Henry VII's foreign policy.

Relations between England and France pre-1485

English kings had been gaining and losing territory in France ever since William the Conqueror had first linked England with the Duchy of Normandy in 1066. Consequently, bitter rivalry had existed between them. The latest contest had been the Hundred Years War (1337–1453), which had resulted in the loss of all English possessions in France except Calais. France had finally been able to drive the English out because of the increasing strength of its monarchy, which had ended civil conflict and absorbed all but one of the **feudatories**. Only Brittany remained, but not for long. Consequently, by the late fifteenth century, France's resources in terms of manpower and revenue were about three times those of its neighbour across the Channel. England could no longer exploit France's weaknesses, nor compete with this enlarged kingdom on equal terms. England's continental ambitions would have to be re-assessed by Henry VII.

Feudatories
Semi-independent territories with feudal lords who owed nominal (in name only) allegiance to the king of France, e.g. Burgundy and Normandy.

England and the unification of Spain

Another factor that influenced the way in which Henry pursued his diplomacy was the unification of Castile and Aragon in 1479, and the consequent arrival of a new power, Spain, on the European stage. In 1494, when the rulers of France and Spain became embroiled in a tussle for control of northern Italy, the main focus of European rivalry changed. Spain assumed England's traditional position as France's main rival, as the theatre of conflict changed from northern to southern Europe and England was relegated to the status of a second-rate power. English kings had no interest in gaining territory in this part of Europe; they also did not have the extra resources available that this would have required. England's role in the Italian wars was that of an occasional ally, adding extra weight to either Spain or France. However, all too often, England was left on the sidelines, and had no share in the rich pickings of victory.

Henry's aims

Key question
What were Henry's aims?

Henry also adopted a more defensive position than that of his predecessors. This was because of the nature of his succession, by usurpation. As we have seen, there were several claimants to his throne who successfully sought aid from foreign powers (see pages 33–41) and Henry had to be constantly on his guard against possible invasion. The most vulnerable part of the kingdom was the northern border with Scotland; as Pope Sixtus V remarked, England was 'only half an island'. Scotland was traditionally the back door into England, and one with which the French were particularly familiar.

Polydore Vergil wrote that Henry was 'more inclined to peace than to war'. The situation in Europe, and initially his own vulnerable position in dynastic and financial terms, made non-intervention on the continent the most sensible approach. Henry's foreign policy was very obviously subordinated to his domestic policies of enriching the monarchy and ensuring the obedience of his subjects. Dynastic threats dominated his dealings with foreign rulers.

When reading the following discussion of Henry's foreign policy it will be important for you to identify Henry's aims and to assess how consistently he pursued them. Following the pattern established by Henry VII's modern biographer, Professor Chrimes, it is customary to divide Henry's foreign policy into three clear phases:

1. 1485–92, culminating in the Treaty of Étaples with France.
2. 1493–1502, which marked the end of the threat from Scotland.
3. 1503 until the king's death in 1509.

2 | 1485–92: Developing Diplomacy

Key question
How did Henry consolidate his support?

Henry's first actions in foreign affairs were deliberately planned to give him time to consolidate support. He had to ensure he had at least nominal support abroad if he was to secure his throne at home. As France had helped to finance the expedition that had led directly to Bosworth, he seized the opportunity to maintain good relations with England's traditional enemy. He immediately negotiated a one-year truce with France that was subsequently extended to January 1489.

Although the Scots had been more favourably disposed towards Henry than Richard at Bosworth, he was aware that the traditional enmity might re-occur once he was the crowned king. Henry desired peace with his northern neighbour, and, in July 1486, he eventually succeeded in persuading James III to agree to a three-year truce. The assassination of James III in 1488 and the accession of the 15-year-old James IV meant that, for a short while at least, Henry had little to fear from across the border.

However, Henry was wise enough to keep his contacts at the Scottish court in case of future aggression.

In spite of the truce with France, in July 1486 Henry negotiated a commercial treaty with Brittany, the other country to offer him hospitality during the long years in exile. Finally, in January 1487 he renewed Edward IV's treaty with Maximilian, king of the Romans, the heir to the Holy Roman Emperor, for one year. So Henry had done his best to ensure that he would not suffer invasion from his principal foreign rivals while he was securing his throne at home. For the time being at least, he was fairly confident that they would not offer assistance to the other claimants to the throne. Perhaps most importantly for Henry, these treaties revealed that he was accepted as king of England by his European counterparts and that they expected him to remain so.

Problems caused by the Simnel rising

Key question
How did Lambert Simnel contribute to Henry VII's problems in foreign policy?

It was the pretender, Lambert Simnel, who led Henry to play a more active role in foreign affairs than he had originally intended. Simnel caused various diplomatic problems because he received support from Ireland and Burgundy, which was still separate from France. The Irish were traditionally opposed to any king of England and were always prepared to support alternative claimants to the English throne. Whereas Irish antagonism was not unusual, that of Burgundy was. Throughout the Hundred Years War against France, Burgundy had been England's main ally. It was also the main outlet for the sale of English cloth. However, Margaret, the Dowager Duchess of Burgundy, the sister of Edward IV, had supported the Yorkists in the recent civil war and was only too willing to provide 2000 mercenaries for Simnel's cause.

Fortunately, other support for Simnel was very limited and Henry was able to defeat the rebels at the battle of Stoke in 1487 (see page 35). However, the episode acted as a warning to Henry, showing how vulnerable his kingship was, particularly when claimants had support from outside the country. It did not threaten any of the recent truces, but it did emphasise the care with which he would have to watch his neighbours.

Brittany

Key question
How significant and successful was Henry's treaty with Brittany?

The first major foreign problem of the reign centred, perhaps not surprisingly, on France. The French king, Charles VIII, was a minor, and the regent was his sister, Anne of Beaujeu. Until 1487 relations between France and England remained harmonious, but hardly had Henry recovered from the Simnel rising when he was forced to take up an aggressive stance towards France.

The situation arose over the future of Brittany. Anne of Beaujeu planned to marry her brother, Charles VIII, to Anne, the daughter and heir of the ageing Duke Francis of Brittany. The French regent was determined to get her way over this because it would be the final stage in her country's long-standing

expansionist policy. Brittany was the only part of the historic kingdom of France that still retained its independence. While Duke Francis was alive the Bretons could try to evade this match. In fact, in 1486 the duke arranged for his daughter to marry Maximilian, who had recently been left a widower on the death of his wife, Mary of Burgundy. He then intrigued with the regent's enemies in France, which provoked her to send an army to Brittany in 1488. Maximilian sent a force of 1500 men to help defend his future father-in-law, and Ferdinand of Aragon, rather begrudgingly, supplied a further 1000. The duke also asked Henry for help, which put the king in a rather awkward position.

Henry VII and the problem of Brittany

Henry explained this predicament to a papal ambassador. The duke had provided him with hospitality throughout his long years in exile (see page 14), so he felt he could not allow France to take over Brittany unopposed. Even had this moral obligation not existed, it would be foolish to allow the French to gain complete control of the southern shore of the Channel, and thus pose an increased threat to England's security. On the other hand, France had also given Henry financial assistance in 1485, and he did not want to jeopardise their fragile truce. So he compromised. He sent several hundred volunteers, under his wife's uncle, Lord Scales, to assist Francis whilst attempting to act as a mediator between the two courts.

However, as the Bretons refused to listen, he renewed the truce with France and disowned Scales. In July 1488 the Bretons were resoundingly defeated by the French at the battle of St Aubin du Cormier. The duke finally capitulated and signed the Treaty of Sablé in which he promised that his daughter would not marry without the permission of the French king, thereby acknowledging himself to be the vassal of the king of France. Three weeks later Duke Francis died (of natural causes) and the 12-year-old Anne became Duchess of Brittany. The French immediately claimed custody of her and the annexation of Brittany by France seemed imminent.

Henry was once again placed in an awkward position. The acquisition of Brittany by France would make England's main rival even more powerful. It would provide valuable bases for an invasion of England, or for the French to attack merchant ships and disrupt English trade. Yet war would severely strain Henry's finances, which he was trying so hard to build up, and would give France an excuse to help the various claimants to the English throne.

Henry prepares for war

Again Henry tried to use diplomacy to save the situation by finding enough allies to deter the French from going to war. He renewed the treaty with Maximilian and, more importantly, made a new alliance with Spain in the Treaty of Medina del Campo in 1489 (see page 145). A treaty was also made with Brittany at Redon in February 1489 in which the Bretons promised to pay

Key terms

Habsburg Empire
Territories ruled
over by the
Habsburg royal
family. These
included Austria,
parts of Germany,
Italy, the
Netherlands and
eventually Spain.

Moors of Granada
Non-Christian
inhabitants of Spain
and Portugal. They
were descendants of
Muslim settlers who
came from north
Africa in the tenth
century.

the cost of the 6000 men Henry undertook to send to them.
Despite this, Henry's policy was still one of restraint, which was
illustrated by the small number of men he intended to send to
Brittany. He also continued to emphasise that he was working
solely to defend England's vital interests, and that he had no
intention of waging a war of conquest.

Henry dispatched the 6000 men to defend Brittany in April
but, despite an initial success at Dixmunde in June where his
force rescued Maximilian's garrison, he found himself let down by
his allies. Maximilian's support was rather unreliable, depending
on his other commitments in the vast **Habsburg Empire** and,
although he married Anne in December 1490, it was only by
proxy (formal promise), which meant that it was not legally
binding. The Spanish sent a force of 2000 in 1490, but they were
recalled before the year was out for service against the **Moors of
Granada**. Finally, in December 1491, the Bretons accepted defeat
and the Duchess Anne was married to King Charles. Their
marriage spelled the end of the independence of Brittany.

Henry now faced one of the most difficult decisions of his
reign. He had promised to go to war against France to defend
Brittany, but Brittany was now officially part of France. It seemed
that Henry had to choose between attempting to liberate
Brittany by conquering France, as Henry V had tried, or leaving
Brittany to her fate while obtaining the best terms he could for
himself. Whichever decision he took there was a real danger that
France would use her increased control of the Channel coast to
invade England.

However, Henry was astute enough to find a more favourable
alternative. While he was aware that England was not strong
enough to challenge France successfully without assistance and
that his allies had proved their unreliability, he recognised that to
withdraw without some show of force would appear weak and
would lose him credibility at home and abroad. He concluded
that an aggressive move might give him the best of both worlds.
It would enhance his reputation and it might have enough
nuisance value to persuade the French to buy him off, just as they
had offered Edward IV generous terms to withdraw his army from
French soil in 1475.

Key question
Why was the Treaty of
Étaples so important
for Henry?

Treaty of Étaples, 1492

Henry announced his intention to assert his claim to the French
crown (since the reign of Edward III (1327–77) kings of England
had consistently claimed to be kings of France also, hence the
Hundred Years War) and sent commissioners to collect a forced
loan when the loss of Brittany seemed imminent in the summer
of 1491. In October he summoned a parliament, which made a
formal grant of two subsidies. Having spent the year preparing
for the invasion of France, the English army, an imposing force
of 26,000 men, crossed the Channel in October 1492 and laid
siege to Boulogne. There they were joined by Breton mercenaries
hired by Henry VII to serve in his invasion force. Because he had
left his departure until late in the campaigning season – armies

rarely fought in winter – it meant that if he did fight it would not be for long.

Fortunately, Charles was eager to be rid of his English aggressor because greater glory was to be won in Italy; so nine days after Henry had set foot on French soil Charles offered peace and on 3 November the Treaty of Étaples was concluded. Charles' only concerns were to keep Brittany and to get rid of Henry. Therefore, he promised to give no further aid to English rebels, particularly Warbeck, and to pay the arrears of the Treaty of Picquigny and most of Henry's costs of intervening in Brittany. This totalled 745,000 gold crowns, payable at the rate of 50,000 crowns a year. In contemporary English currency this equalled about £5000, approximately five per cent of the king's annual income.

Henry had not won a glorious victory, for the independence of Brittany was gone forever and the whole of the southern side of the Channel, apart from Calais, was now in French hands. However, the outcome had not been completely negative. He had prevented Charles VIII from helping Perkin Warbeck and he had secured a sizeable annual pension from the French. Whilst contending with French aggression he had made a valuable alliance with Spain and had also shown that England under a Tudor king could not be completely overlooked in continental affairs. Perhaps it would be unreasonable to expect Henry to have achieved more, given the situation in which he found himself.

Treaty of Medina del Campo, 1489

The most significant achievement of Henry VII's foreign policy was the alliance negotiated with Spain in the Treaty of Medina del Campo signed in March 1489. Spain emerged as a major power in the late fifteenth century after the unification of the country in 1479. Initially England and Spain were commercial rivals, but both were willing to sink their differences in a common animosity towards France.

Early in 1488 Henry suggested a **betrothal** between his eldest son, Prince Arthur, and Ferdinand and Isabella's youngest daughter, Catherine of Aragon, when they reached marriageable age. Catherine, then aged three, was six months older than her intended husband. The negotiations were laborious as both fathers wanted to secure the best possible terms. Finally, Ferdinand agreed to Henry's demands about the size of Catherine's **dowry** and promised not to help any English rebels.

It was more difficult to reach agreement over relations with France. In the end it was specified that if either country found itself at war with France, the other was to intervene immediately. War was obviously expected in the near future, particularly by the Spanish. Their objective was the reconquest from France of the Pyrenean territories of Cerdagne and Rousillon, and in return they promised Henry help in his regaining Normandy and Aquitaine. However, this was not realistic, for, although the French might be persuaded to relinquish the Pyrenean territories

Key question
How significant an achievement for Henry was the treaty of Medina del Campo?

Key terms

Betrothal
Promise of marriage made between parents on behalf of their children.

Dowry
Money or property paid by the bride's father on his daughter's marriage.

Profile: Ferdinand and Isabella

1451	– Isabella born in Castile, Spain. Daughter and heiress to King John II
1452	– Ferdinand born in Aragon, Spain. Eldest son of King John II of Aragon
1469	– Ferdinand and Isabella married
1474	– Isabella succeeded her half-brother King Henry IV as ruler of Castile
1474–79	– Ferdinand and Isabella fought for control of Castile in civil war. They were opposed by nobility who refused to accept Isabella as their queen
1479	– Ferdinand succeeded his father as king of Aragon
1489	– Ferdinand and Isabella signed treaty of Medina del Campo with Henry VII of England
	– They agreed to the marriage of their daughter Catherine with Henry VII's eldest son Arthur
1492	– Ferdinand and Isabella conquered Granada and thus united the whole of Spain under their rule.
1504	– Isabella died.
1504–7	– Ferdinand temporarily lost control of Castile in a civil war provoked by the death of his wife.
1516	– Ferdinand died

which lay outside their 'natural boundaries', they were most unlikely ever to contemplate the loss of Normandy or Aquitaine which were regarded as integral parts of the country. It certainly appears that Henry had the worst of the bargain.

By 1493 the Catholic kings had achieved their aim in the Pyrenees, while doing little to help Henry accomplish his. But Henry himself does not seem to have felt this, or else he chose to ignore it, and continued his pro-Spanish policy throughout his reign. Perhaps this was because for Henry his triumph lay in his being recognised as an equal by one of the leading royal families of Europe. This was of major importance to a usurper who was desperately keen to secure international recognition of the legitimacy of his position as king. He celebrated his success by having a new gold sovereign minted on which he was portrayed wearing not the traditional open crown of England, but the more prestigious imperial crown closed over with hoops.

Summary diagram: Europe 1485–92

```
                        ┌─────────────────────────┐
                        │      Europe in 1485      │
                        └─────────────────────────┘
              ┌──────────────────┐          ┌──────────────┐
              │ Rivalry between  │          │ Unification  │
              │ France and England│         │     of       │
              │    pre-1485      │          │    Spain     │
              └──────────────────┘          └──────────────┘

  ┌─────────────────────────────────────────────────────────────┐
  │ 1485          Developing diplomacy                      1492 │
  └─────────────────────────────────────────────────────────────┘
```

| Truces: France 1485 Scotland 1486 | 1487 | 1487–92 | 1489 | 1492 |
| Treaty: Holy Roman Empire 1487 | Lambert Simnel rising | Problem of Brittany's independence | Treaty of Medina del Campo | Treaty of Étaples |

3 | 1493–1502: Successful Diplomacy

Key question
How successful was Henry's diplomacy during this period?

This period was Henry's most successful in diplomatic affairs. Initially this was a result of Charles VIII's successes in Italy. The other European rulers feared that France was becoming too powerful and in 1495 the Pope, Ferdinand, Maximilian, Venice and Milan formed the League of Venice with the aim of driving Charles out of Italy. England was not included because the theatre of conflict was outside the country's usual sphere of interest, but by 1496 Ferdinand had realised that it might be dangerous to exclude England. Perhaps he suspected that Henry wished to preserve good relations with France and was fearful of losing England's goodwill. Certainly Charles appeared to be ingratiating himself with Henry by offering practical assistance against Warbeck (see pages 36–7).

Whatever the reason, in October 1496 Ferdinand and Henry concluded a further agreement for the marriage of Catherine and Arthur. Also in the same year Ferdinand secured England's entry into the revamped League of Venice, now called the Holy League. However, Henry showed that he was no-one's puppet by joining the League only on condition that England was not bound to go to war against France. Ferdinand agreed to this because England's neutrality was preferable to an alliance with France. To Henry's credit he also managed to make a commercial treaty with France while maintaining good relations with his allies in the League. So 1496 was a successful year for Henry, particularly as he also concluded the *Magnus Intercursus*, the basis on which good trading relations were resumed between England and Burgundy (see page 126).

Key date

Henry joined the anti-French alliance known as the League of Venice: 1495 (later re-named the Holy League: 1496)

Key question
How did the Warbeck rising affect relations with other powers?

Warbeck rising

The following year, 1497, saw Warbeck finally captured and peace made with Scotland. The significance of Warbeck's career to Henry in the field of foreign affairs was that he involved other rulers in England's dynastic problem. Warbeck received support at different times from Ireland, France, Burgundy and Scotland. This greatly complicated Henry's foreign policy and at times jeopardised key features of it. This was particularly evident over the treaty with Spain as the Catholic kings did not wish their daughter to marry the heir to an insecure crown (see pages 145–6). A further example was in 1493 when Henry went as far as disrupting England's cloth trade by placing a temporary embargo on commercial dealings with the Netherlands because Philip and Margaret were offering Warbeck aid. It also highlighted the long-term problem of possible invasion of England via Scotland.

Truce of Ayton, 1497

Relations between Scotland and England were always tense, with the Scots taking any opportunity to cross the border and cause problems for their overlord, the King of England. The kings of Scotland traditionally owed allegiance to the English kings, although they resented this and were always looking for ways to avoid it. James IV of Scotland was no exception to the rule and, despite a truce made with Henry when he came to the throne in 1488, he took Perkin Warbeck into his favour when he arrived in Scotland in 1495. He even went as far as to give Warbeck his cousin in marriage, which must have appeared extremely threatening to Henry. However, Warbeck's invasion of England with Scottish help came to nothing; he gained no support south of the border and, when the Scots heard that Henry was sending an army to oppose them, they took flight.

For Henry the situation was made worse by the simultaneous outbreak of a rebellion in Cornwall (see pages 31–2). The people resented having to pay for an invasion which was unlikely to affect them. Fortunately, James IV was losing faith in Warbeck and he did not take advantage of this rebellion to launch another attack of his own. Henry was now able to offer terms on which a treaty with Scotland could be based. The truce of Ayton was concluded in 1497, but it was not until Warbeck had been executed that it became a full treaty of peace. This was a great achievement for Henry as no such agreement had been reached between the two countries since 1328. The treaty was sealed by the marriage of James to Margaret, Henry's eldest daughter, in August 1503. However, Scotland did not abandon her ancient pact with France; this meant that the peace depended on the continuation of good relations between England and France, but while Henry lived this did not pose a problem.

Key question
What did Henry VII hope to gain from the marriage of Prince Arthur?

Marriage of Prince Arthur and Catherine of Aragon

Another of Henry's diplomatic marriage alliances was also achieved in this period. In October 1501 Catherine of Aragon arrived in England with 100,000 crowns of her dowry. On 14 November she and Arthur were married in St Paul's Cathedral. This alliance was now of even greater significance than when it had originally been mooted. Not only did Henry hope that England would play a part in the growing Spanish empire in the New World, but the marriage of Catherine's sister, Joanna, to Philip of Burgundy tied their two countries closer together and provided Henry with the possibility of another ally if he were to need one. The two marriage alliances were the pinnacle of Henry's success in his foreign policy.

Arthur marries Catherine of Aragon: 1501

Key date

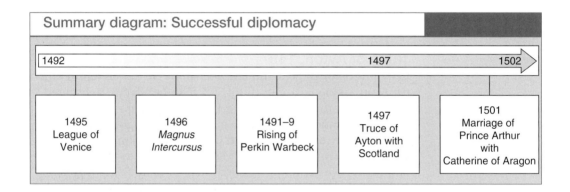

Summary diagram: Successful diplomacy

1492			1497		1502
1495 League of Venice	1496 *Magnus Intercursus*	1491–9 Rising of Perkin Warbeck	1497 Truce of Ayton with Scotland		1501 Marriage of Prince Arthur with Catherine of Aragon

4 | 1503–9: Changing Diplomacy

This third and final period of Henry's foreign policy was marred by dynastic upsets and changes in Europe that acted against England's interests.

Death of Prince Arthur

The major blow to Henry's policy was the sudden death of Prince Arthur at Ludlow in April 1502, only five months after his wedding. It seemed that Henry's dynastic hopes had been shattered, but within five weeks of Arthur's death Ferdinand and Isabella were instructing their ambassador to conclude a marriage with Prince Henry, the new heir to the throne, and to settle the terms of the dowry. A formal treaty was confirmed in September 1502, but it recognised that a dispensation would be needed from the Pope because Catherine was related to Henry in the **first degree of affinity** because of her marriage to Arthur. The required document arrived in 1504 but by then the diplomatic situation had moved on.

Key question
How did Arthur's death have an impact on foreign policy?

First degree of affinity
Close relation, usually first cousins.

Key term

Death of Queen Elizabeth

In February 1503 Henry suffered another personal loss when his wife, Queen Elizabeth, died shortly after giving birth to a daughter. This provoked new dynastic worries. Two of Henry's

Key question
Why did Elizabeth's death make Henry vulnerable?

three sons were already dead, and with the death of his wife he had no hope of more children to come. As if to emphasise Henry's vulnerable position, Edmund de la Pole chose this time to flee abroad (see pages 40–1).

Henry began to consider the possibility of taking a second wife who might be able to bear him more heirs; he seems to have sought the hand of Joanna of Naples, Margaret of Savoy and Joanna of Castile and Burgundy in turn. The once-popular idea that he intended to marry his daughter-in-law, Catherine of Aragon, can be dismissed as it is not based on any firm evidence. His first choice in 1504 seems to have been the young widow, Queen Joanna of Naples, the niece of Ferdinand of Aragon. This match was encouraged by Spain because Ferdinand was keen to strengthen his links with England as his relations with France were worsening. However, this possibility came to nothing because of a third significant death, that of Isabella of Castile, later in 1504.

Death of Isabella

Key question
What effect did Isabella's death have on European relations?

Queen Isabella's death did not just mean that Henry and Ferdinand were now rivals in the matrimonial stakes, it also threw into question the continued unity of Spain because of the position of Castile. Joanna was her mother's heir to the kingdom, so the unity of Spain could only be preserved if she allowed her father to act as regent on her behalf. However, Joanna's husband, Philip of Burgundy, dazzled by the prospect of a crown to add to his other titles, forced her to take up her inheritance immediately. It therefore appeared to Henry that his major ally might be reduced in status from king of the whole of Spain to that of Aragon. In addition, his two allies, Spain and Burgundy, on whom he depended in case of enmity from France, were now rivals. Henry had to struggle hard to ensure that he lost the support of neither. This explains why in the last few years of his life his foreign policy was subject to sudden changes of direction in a way that it had never been before.

Relations with Burgundy

Key question
Why did England's relations with Burgundy change?

In 1505 Henry attempted to establish more amicable relations with Philip in case of a possible break with France. He also wanted to ensure better trading links with Antwerp and to persuade Philip to surrender the Earl of Suffolk (see pages 40–1). Friendship with Philip at this time automatically made relations with Ferdinand more difficult, particularly after Henry had lent Philip money to finance his expedition to claim the throne of Castile. Henry also considered marrying Margaret of Savoy, the daughter of Maximilian and sister of Philip, which jeopardised the prospective marriage of Prince Henry and Catherine of Aragon. Henry further antagonised Ferdinand by keeping the Princess' dowry, despite her father's requests to complete the marriage settlement or return the bride and her dowry to Spain. The young Prince Henry was even persuaded to register a formal protest that a marriage with the widow of his brother was against his conscience.

Henry VII now began to seek a French or a Burgundian bride for his son. In 1506 Philip was forced to take shelter at the English court because of a violent storm at sea and Henry seized this opportunity to negotiate a treaty with him. This stated that Suffolk should be handed over to the English and that his son, Prince Henry, would marry Philip's sister. Finding himself isolated, Ferdinand sought an agreement with France, as Louis XII was glad to see the union between Spain and the Netherlands shattered. This was cemented in October 1505 when Ferdinand married Germaine de Foix, Louis' niece.

Restoration of links with Spain

However, the diplomatic scene was completely altered in September 1506 when Philip of Burgundy died. His wife, Joanna, supposedly went mad with grief and this provided Ferdinand with an excuse to take over Castile. In the Netherlands, Margaret of Savoy acted as Regent for her nephew, the six-year-old Archduke Charles (the son of Joanna and Philip), although control really lay with her father, Maximilian. Henry's diplomacy had to alter

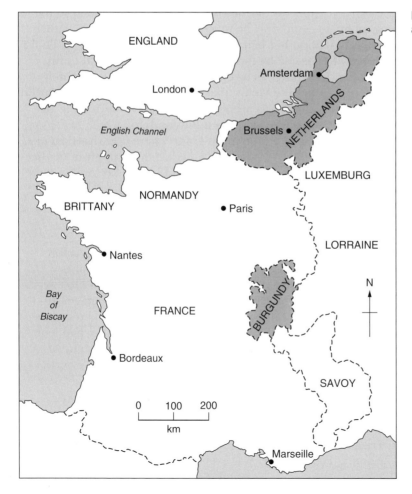

Figure 7.2: Burgundy and the Netherlands

direction rapidly to keep pace with these changes. Fearing that France would seize upon the weakness of the Netherlands to take lands there, Henry tried to restore links with Ferdinand and to strengthen relations with Maximilian.

Margaret of Savoy had rejected his proposal of marriage as she wished to remain a widow, so Henry now sought Joanna of Castile as his wife, believing that the rumours of her madness had been circulated by her father merely as a pretext by which to gain control of Castile. It was a desperate bid to maintain the triangular alliance of England, Castile and Burgundy against France. However it was now Ferdinand in the advantageous position. He was in control of Castile and allied with France, so he refused to agree to Joanna's marriage or to send the rest of Catherine's dowry.

Key question
What was the League of Cambrai?

League of Cambrai, 1508

Henry decided that his earlier hope of a triple alliance of England, Castile and Burgundy was unworkable in the existing political climate. Therefore he tried to form a three-way agreement between England, the Netherlands and France. He showed that he was serious about this by revoking the *Malus Intercursus* and reinstating the *Magnus Intercursus* (see page 126).

Profile: Richard Fox 1448–1528

c. 1448	– Born near Grantham in Lincolnshire
c. 1460s	– Educated at Winchester and Magdalen College, Oxford
c. 1470s	– Studied theology in Paris where he met Henry Tudor
1484–5	– Negotiated with the French for financial and military support for Henry's invasion of England
1485	– Appointed to Henry VII's ruling Council as Lord Privy Seal
1486	– Appointed the king's Principal Secretary
1487	– Appointed Bishop of Exeter
1492	– Promoted to bishopric of Bath and Wells
1494	– Promoted to bishopric of Durham. Chief English envoy in the treaty of Étaples
1496	– Negotiated *Magnus Intercursus*
1497	– Helped repel the invasion of the Scots and negotiated the treaty of Ayton
1501	– Promoted to bishopric of Winchester
1508	– Negotiated alliance with Archduke Charles (later Charles V)

Fox was a member of the king's close circle of friends and advisers. He arranged the marriages of Henry's children – Margaret married James IV of Scotland, Arthur married Catherine of Aragon – and was the leading foreign diplomat in the king's service.

This was intended to placate the Netherlands, although it was clearly contrary to England's trading interests. Then in December 1507 Maximilian was prevailed upon to agree to a marriage between the young Archduke Charles (eldest son of Philip of Burgundy and Joanna of Castile) and Henry's younger daughter, Mary. Henry made a further attempt to win the hand of Margaret of Savoy, but was again unsuccessful. In an attempt to discomfit Ferdinand even more, he offered Prince Henry as husband for Louis XII's niece, Margaret of Angoulême.

By 1508 it seemed as though Henry's dream of uniting his Habsburg and French allies against Ferdinand might become a reality. The unifying factor was to be the League of Cambrai, ostensibly planned to finance a crusade against the Turks, but in reality designed to be an anti-Spanish alliance. However, at the eleventh hour Louis XII decided that he dare not jeopardise his understanding with Ferdinand over Italy, and he bribed the Spanish king to join him. So when the League of Cambrai was signed in December 1508 it was as an alliance against Venice, between the Pope, Louis XII, Maximilian, the Archduke Charles and Ferdinand. In the end it was Henry, and not his wily Spanish rival, who was left isolated by this alliance. However, all these rulers continued to express their support for Henry, and the League did not threaten any of England's vital interests. In fact it had the advantage of turning Europe's attention away from England at a time when Henry VII was nearing the end of his life.

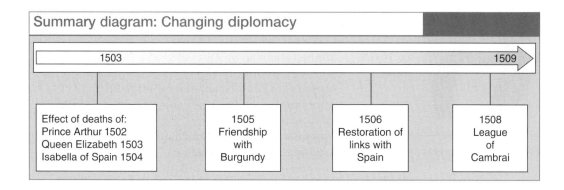

Summary diagram: Changing diplomacy

1503 — 1509

| Effect of deaths of: Prince Arthur 1502 Queen Elizabeth 1503 Isabella of Spain 1504 | 1505 Friendship with Burgundy | 1506 Restoration of links with Spain | 1508 League of Cambrai |

5 | The Key Debate

How successful was Henry's foreign policy?

Polydore Vergil wrote that Henry 'was most fortunate in war, although he was constitutionally more inclined to peace than to war'. The first part of this statement does not seem to fit with what we know of the Breton crisis and subsequent 'war' with France, the only one which he waged. However, the second half rings true. The king did pursue a policy of peace, even if he could not do so consistently because of the fluid nature of Renaissance diplomacy.

Henry was cautious by nature, but he was also forced by circumstances to pursue a peaceful policy because it was less expensive, and he lacked the resources to defeat his continental neighbours on their own soil. This was why he was prepared to sign the Treaty of Étaples with the French king after he had barely set foot in France. It was not a glamorous policy, but it was probably the only one that had a realistic chance of being successful.

The other factor that constantly influenced the direction of Henry's foreign policy was the need to protect his newly founded dynasty from foreign-supported rebellion. Many of his negotiations with foreign powers, particularly those with Burgundy, were aimed at cutting off support from challengers to his throne and he was generally successful in his attempts. The marriage alliance with Scotland at least temporarily removed one source of potential support for those who wished to challenge his right to be king.

However, it was the Treaty of Medina del Campo signed with Spain that was Henry's major achievement in foreign affairs, even though its gains were temporarily threatened towards the end of his reign. This treaty not only confirmed the recognition of the Tudor dynasty by one of the most powerful European states, thus eliminating yet another potential source of support for rival claimants to his throne, but it also opened up the realistic possibility of an effective anti-French partnership. The fact that Ferdinand's deviousness and unreliability as an ally meant that an Anglo-Spanish 'axis' never properly developed should not detract from the credit Henry deserves for spotting its potential and playing his part in trying to establish it.

It is clear that the main principles which guided Henry's foreign policy were peace whenever possible, because of his concern not to spend money unnecessarily, and the protection of his regime from foreign-backed challenges. However, it should not be imagined that these were carefully conceived approaches from the start. They emerged as the reign progressed and as it became obvious that they were the most sensible policies to pursue. Nor should it be thought that these were his only concerns, although his desires to advance the cause of English trade and to continue the traditional rivalry with France were almost always kept subservient to his major aims.

Equally, it would be unwise to lay too much emphasis on the coherence or consistency of his diplomacy. For example, the deaths of key figures in his own and other royal families in the first years of the sixteenth century meant that he could not pursue an unswerving policy, and they tested his flexibility and resourcefulness to the full. It was to his credit that he was generally found equal to the challenge. In 1509 Henry could be well pleased with the results of his diplomacy. England was on good terms with most of Europe, his dynasty was secure and was recognised by other rulers, and, most importantly, all this had been achieved without draining his treasury of its hard-won resources.

Study Guide: AS Questions

In the style of AQA

Study the following source and then answer the questions that follow.

Henry's diplomacy was more concerned with peace than war. His own experience before and in 1485 would have made him only too well aware of the importance of foreign support for anyone who hoped to gain the throne. The marriages of his children strengthened diplomatic links.

(a) Comment on 'the importance of foreign support' in the context of the struggle for the throne in 1485.   (3 marks)

(b) Explain why the marriages of Henry VII's children 'strengthened diplomatic links' with other kingdoms in the years 1485–1503.   (7 marks)

(c) How important, in relation with other factors, was the need for security in explaining Henry VII's foreign policy between 1485 and 1509?   (15 marks)

Source: AQA, 2003

Exam tips

The cross-references are intended to take you straight to the material that will help you to answer the questions.

1. In question **(a)** you must highlight the importance of foreign support for Henry's bid for the throne, for example:

    - The French provided Henry with support in the shape of ships and mercenaries (pages 12–15).
    - Breton mercenaries were hired to serve in Henry's invasion force (page 15).

2. In question **(b)** you have to explain why the marriage of Henry's children strengthened England's diplomatic links, for example:

    - The marriage between Arthur and Catherine of Aragon strengthened England's trade and political links with Spain (pages 144–5).
    - The marriage between Margaret and James IV of Scotland secured England's northern border and prevented Scottish aid for the pretender Warbeck (page 147).
    - The marriages with foreign powers added to the prestige and stability of the Tudor dynasty.

3. In question **(c)** you should evaluate the extent to which Henry's need for security dominated his foreign policy when compared to other factors such as trade and prestige. You should show how Henry's priorities shifted between security and other factors throughout his reign, for example:

    - Henry's treaties with Spain and Scotland show that security was a very important part of his foreign policy (pages 144–7).
    - Henry's treaties with Burgundy and France show how important trade and prestige were to a newly crowned king (pages 143–4 and 149–50).

In the style of Edexcel

Study Sources 1–5 below and answer questions (a)–(e) that follow on page 157.

Source 1

From: the Treaty of Medina del Campo between England and Spain, March 1489.

A true friendship and alliance shall be observed henceforth between Ferdinand and Isabella, their heirs and subjects, on the one part, and Henry, his heirs and successors, on the other part. They promise to assist one another in defending their present and future dominions against any enemy whatsoever.

Both countries agree to help one another to defend their lands against any enemy. The people of each country are allowed to live in one another's countries and to trade there. Neither country shall give any help to rebels from the other country, or allow them to remain in their lands.

Source 2

Extracts from letters written by King Ferdinand and Queen Isabella to the Spanish Ambassador in England, de Puebla, 10–15 January 1497.

We have read your letter and think that you have acted correctly concerning the marriage treaty. We know that King Henry has asked the Pope to allow the marriage even though the parties are young. Everything has been done as it should be … Speak to the King about the marriage. You should insist that there must be an alliance and we look to you to improve the terms of the treaty. The duties on goods brought into England from Spain should be lowered. If the King will not agree, then we will raise duties on English goods here.

Source 3

Letter from Queen Isabella to the Spanish Ambassador in England, the Duke de Estrada, 12 July 1502.

It is vital that there should be no delay in making an agreement for the marriage of the Princess of Wales, our daughter, to the new Prince of Wales. This is now even more urgent since we hear that the King of France is trying to stop the marriage.

After the marriage, our anxiety will cease and we will be able to get England's help in our war against France. Let King Henry know that the King of France is sending a force against us. Henry knows that, under the terms of the treaty signed between us, England and Spain agree to defend each other's possessions. So try to get King Henry to take part in our war with France. Tell him that we will never have such a good chance again of recovering his territories in France.

Source 4

A picture showing Henry VII with his wife and Prince Henry with his wife Princess Catherine. It also shows St George and the Dragon. It was painted between 1503 and 1509. The picture is in the Royal Collection at Windsor.

Source 5

From: Roger Lockyer and Dan O'Sullivan, Tudor Britain, 1485–1603, *1997.*

Henry VII's major concern was to secure his throne and his succession against a series of claimants – in particular Lambert Simnel (1486–7) and Perkin Warbeck (1491–9), each of whom received support from foreign powers. In other words, dynastic threats dominated Henry's dealings with foreign rulers … There is no doubt, too, that Henry was obsessed by the problems of internal security throughout his reign, because his original claim to the throne had been so weak. He relied on a network of agents and informers. By the end of his reign Henry VII had eliminated a series of dangerous pretenders, had been recognized as King by the other major rulers, and had strengthened his dynasty by arranging that Catherine of Aragon, following the death of Prince Arthur, should marry the future Henry VIII.

(a) Study Source 1

What can you learn from Source 1 about the aims of the Spanish rulers in their negotiations with Henry VII in 1497?

(6 marks)

(b) Use your own knowledge

Use your own knowledge to explain in what ways 'Lambert Simnel' and 'Perkin Warbeck' threatened Henry VII.

(10 marks)

(c) Study Sources 1 and 5

What evidence in Source 1 supports the view of the authors of Source 5 that 'dynastic threats dominated Henry's dealings with foreign powers'?

(10 marks)

(d) Study Sources 3 and 4

How useful are these two sources to an historian studying the importance of royal marriages to the stability of the monarchy in the reign of Henry VII?

(10 marks)

(e) Study Sources 3 and 5 and use your own knowledge

Do you agree that foreign support was the central reason why Henry VII was able to 'secure the throne'? Explain your answer, using the sources and your own knowledge.

(24 marks)

Source: Edexcel, 2000

Exam tips

The cross-references are intended to take you straight to the material that will help you to answer the questions.

1. The answer to question **(a)** is to be found entirely within Source 1. You have to show that you have understood the content of the source. You do not have to use your own knowledge but you should comment on what the source implies. Keep your answer to the point, for example Spain was keen to secure:

   • an ally to assist in its defence should it be attacked
   • a trading partner.

2. In question **(b)** you must use your own knowledge to explain the ways in which the pretenders Simnel and Warbeck threatened Henry VII, for example:

   • They threatened his life and the lives of his family.
   • They threatened the security of the dynasty and the stability of the kingdom.
   • They threatened to involve England in a war against its more powerful continental neighbours.

3. In question **(c)** you have to understand what is being said in Sources 1 and 5. Evaluate the extent to which Source 1 supports (or not) the view of the historians in Source 5, for example:

   • The reference to not giving aid to 'rebels' in Source 1 supports the views expressed in Source 5.
   • The references to 'defence' and 'the enemy' may also be used to support the views expressed in Source 5.

4. In question **(d)** you have to focus on the key word 'useful' and suggest ways in which an historian might find Sources 3 and 4 useful in studying the importance of royal marriages to the stability of the monarchy. How far can the sources be trusted to give an accurate picture of events? For example:

    - Source 3 suggests that marriage was a vital factor in maintaining the friendship and support of Spain.
    - Source 4 suggests that the royal family were content, confident and stable. The painting was useful propaganda designed to show the stability of the royal family and the security of the dynasty.
    - On the other hand, you might argue that the pressure to maintain the marriage alliance with Spain could easily have involved Henry in a war with his nearest neighbour, France. The uncertainties of war could easily affect the stability of the monarchy.

5. Question **(e)** carries the greatest number of marks, so deserves the greatest amount of time devoted to it.

    - You have to recall your own knowledge in order to discuss the means by which Henry secured the throne.
    - You must assess the contribution foreign support made to securing the throne by reference to the sources, the contents of which are there to help you. (You must resist the temptation to copy the source content but specific quotation is permissible if it is used to support a point you are trying to make.)
    - You must also show how his other policies – in government, in finance and in respect of the nobility – also contributed to securing the throne (pages 24–42).
    - You should round off your answer by offering an opinion in respect of how far you agree or disagree with the question.

In the style of OCR

(a) Assess the claim that the most important achievement of Henry VII's foreign policy was to defeat any threat to a Tudor succession. (45 marks)

Source: OCR, 2002

(b) To what extent was Henry VII's foreign policy motivated by financial considerations? (45 marks)

Exam tips

The cross-references are intended to take you straight to the material that will help you to answer the questions.

1. In question **(a)** you should focus on and assess an interpretation of foreign policy. You must consider the succession alongside other achievements, which should be compared and evaluated before coming to a balanced conclusion. For example, although the defeat of the threat to a Tudor succession was an important achievement of Henry VII's foreign policy (pages 139–53), there were other achievements, for example:

   - To secure the recognition of foreign rulers.
   - To enhance trade.
   - To cut off aid and thus weaken the pretenders.
   - To secure marriage alliances.

2. In question **(b)** you must compare and evaluate the reason mentioned (financial considerations) in the question with other equally relevant reasons rather than simply offer a descriptive list of causes. Therefore, you should consider the extent to which Henry VII's foreign policy was motivated by other factors aside from finance. For example, although the French pension and the financial settlement received from the King of Spain on the marriage of Arthur and Catherine of Aragon suggest that financial gain was at the heart of Henry's foreign policy (pages 139–53), other equally important motivating factors need to be considered, for example:

   - To secure the throne and dynasty (pages 24–43).
   - To enhance Henry's status and prestige (pages 24–43).

---

8 Henry's Legacy: History's Verdict on Henry VII

POINTS TO CONSIDER
This chapter draws together themes that have been dealt with separately in each earlier chapter. It explores the way in which historians have changed their views on Henry and whether or not he achieved his aims. These are examined in three themes:

- History's treatment of Henry VII
- The 'new monarchy' theory
- Did Henry achieve his aims?

1 | History's Treatment of Henry VII

Earlier historians

The views of historians on the achievements of Henry VII have varied over the centuries. The judgements of earlier historians were influenced by the traditional assessment of the fifteenth century, which was hampered by inadequate knowledge and coloured by a distorted view of this period in English history as superstitious and uncivilised. For example, Edward Hall published his *Chronicle* in 1547 and entitled it 'The union of the two noble and illustrious families of Lancaster and York, being long in continual dissension for the crown of this noble realm'. He saw Henry as the saviour of England after the civil strife that had dogged the country since Henry IV's usurpation in 1399. Shakespeare continued this theme in his history plays making Henry VII's main aim 'to unite the white rose and the red'.

One of the most influential assessments of Henry's reign was *The Life of Henry VII* by Francis Bacon, first published in 1622. His praise for Henry was probably intended to gain the favour of Henry's descendant, James I, as the picture he paints of Henry is similar to how James saw himself. It is from Bacon that such memorable phrases as 'a wonder for wise men', and 'this Solomon of England' spring. Bacon saw Henry as master of his own realm and 'arbiter in Europe'. This **eulogy** misled later historians and

> **Key question**
> How have historians modified their views of Henry VII?

> **Eulogy**
> Something written in praise of a person.
>
> *Key term*

led them to exaggerate Henry's achievements. By the late nineteenth century the 'new monarchy' theory had arisen. This was the belief that Henry, having rescued England from the ravages of civil war, proceeded dynamically to restructure the government of the country. He was cast as an innovator in the art of government.

Modern historians

Today, with more extensive research available on the later middle ages, Henry's methods of government seem far less revolutionary and, in fact, very similar to those of his Yorkist predecessors. The most outstanding work written in the twentieth century is the study of Henry's reign by S.B. Chrimes. He argues that Henry was an essentially medieval monarch but that he gave England the stability it needed after the Wars of the Roses. Chrimes is supported in his conclusions by John Guy and John Lander.

However, Christine Carpenter has recently cast doubt on Henry's achievements. Describing herself as an 'unrepentant critic of the king', she suggests that the question of whether Henry should be described as a 'medieval' or 'modern' king is irrelevant. She has concentrated on his so-called achievements which she believes have been exaggerated. For example, she believes that in favouring a minority of nobles Henry undermined law and order because they got away with breaking the law while others were severely punished. This threatened the stability of the kingdom. Dr Carpenter's views are not shared by all historians.

Clearly, in order to assess how consistent and successful Henry was, it is necessary for students of early Tudor history to make up their own minds by:

- Understanding what Henry's aims were.
- Assessing whether or not he resorted to well-tried methods.
- Assessing whether or not his reign marked a 'new' beginning.

2 | The Key Debate

It was generally agreed from the end of the nineteenth century until quite recently that 1485 marked the beginning of the period called the 'new monarchy' in English history. Historians took Henry VII's reign as the starting point of this period because they identified his rule with the end of the turmoil of the Wars of the Roses and the establishment of a strong, efficient monarchy. They argued that late medieval government had been developing well. They typified it as a system with the monarch at the centre, ruling by consultation with his higher subjects, with a highly developed and respected legal system and with the freedom of the people recognised by the summoning of parliament. They believed that the civil strife of the mid-fifteenth century severely interrupted this progress and that government lost its direction until the accession of Henry VII.

The establishment of a new and highly successful dynasty seemed the obvious place to start, particularly within the wider context of Europe and with all the dramatic changes brought about by the Renaissance. Historians today challenge this interpretation. They argue that Henry's reign was not so much new and innovative, as essentially medieval in character. Now that more extensive research has been carried out on the government of the Yorkist kings it is easier to see similarities with the government of the first Tudor. Let us review the main features of Henry's reign in the context of the former emphasis on change and the more recent stress on continuity and ask the question:

> Did Henry VII's reign mark the beginning of a new age in English history?

Historians who supported the new monarchy theory emphasised the fact that Henry restored the solvency of the crown, rescuing it from the poverty of the civil war. The implication was that he achieved this by employing 'modern' as opposed to 'medieval' approaches.

Finance

It cannot now be maintained that his financial policy was in any sense revolutionary. It is clear that he stretched all the existing sources of revenue to their limit, so that he was not only solvent, but had enough savings to make him confident that his son's succession would be assured. But it would be difficult to escape the conclusion that Henry's sources of revenue were not new, and that they were the traditional methods of raising money, familiar to every later medieval king. Where, of course, he was different was in the way he exploited these sources. Through painstaking and meticulous attention to detail he utilised them to the full. For example, his own auditing of the accounts was unique in an English ruler and added greatly to the efficiency of the system.

Nobility

Another policy of Henry's that was reputedly 'new' was his thrusting of the nobility from their traditional role as advisers of the monarch and replacing them with lesser men. This was not the case. A considerable number of peers served on Henry's council and they were certainly not deliberately overlooked when he needed advice. In fact some, such as the Earl of Oxford and Duke of Bedford, were amongst his closest friends and servants. However, where Henry did differ from tradition was that he did not rely on a handful of favoured magnates. Above all else, he demanded ability and loyalty in his advisers and he promoted men on those criteria alone, rather than giving priority to those with the highest social status. Oxford, Bray, Morton, Empson and Dudley came from a variety of backgrounds; but what they had in common was that they attained high office and remained there because they served their master and their country well.

A further charge made against Henry in his supposedly 'new' treatment of the nobility was that he exploited them financially,

Key question
Did Henry treat the nobility differently to previous kings?

particularly in the later years of the reign. Certainly they, more than any other section of society, were forced to pay huge sums of money to the king, but it is important to establish why this was so. It was not, as those historians who support the 'new monarchy' theory have argued, a further attempt to destroy the power of the peerage. It is true that Henry realised from his own experiences of the Wars of the Roses how dominant the nobility had become during a period of civil war in which the power of the monarch had largely withered away.

However, he also understood that its continued existence as a powerful force was vital to the maintenance of social order as he understood it. So his intention was to restore the nobility to its 'proper place' as the leaders of society under the crown. Like Edward IV, he saw that one of the ways in which this could be achieved was by tackling the problems posed by livery and maintenance. However, unlike his predecessor, he allowed no-one to ignore these laws and consequently was much more successful in dealing with the problem. At the same time, he also knew that if he was to use his most powerful subjects to impose law and order in the country at large, he must be able to rely on their loyalty. The system of bonds and recognisances that was used so extensively was primarily intended to achieve this aim. He had no intention of financially crippling any lord who was loyal to the regime.

Law and order

Key question
Did Henry achieve law and order?

Earlier historians emphasised the achievement of Henry in restoring law and order after society had been shattered by the insurrections of the mid-fifteenth century. His achievement in this field was certainly impressive for the period, but it should be remembered that the ways in which he set about settling this problem were very similar to those used by Edward IV – the limiting of livery and maintenance, the development of the role of the JPs in the localities and the establishment of provincial councils.

However, there was one major difference. Although Henry's methods were not new, they were pursued more vigorously than ever before. His act against livery and maintenance broke down local power bases built up by ambitious nobles in the past. This, together with his general policy of asserting his rights over the higher nobility, encouraged lesser peers and the major non-noble families to turn to him for support when they were threatened by a social superior. Thus, for the first time, the crown became the judge in most disputes between members of the élite groups.

Government

Key question
Did government change in the reign of Henry VII?

Another feature traditionally identified as part of the new Tudor monarchy was the beginning of government through the household, rather than through the long-established institutions of government. One important piece of evidence that was used to support this argument was Henry's decision quite early in the reign to make the Chamber, rather than the Exchequer, the major financial department of state. But again, later research has shown that there was nothing new in this. Edward IV had successfully used the Chamber for this purpose, and Henry was merely following his example. Early historians were deceived by the fact that at the beginning of his reign Henry's methods of government were necessarily traditional as his experience of kingship was so limited.

Therefore, initially he used the Exchequer to deal with his revenue and adopted a consultative style of government. He conciliated the peers by consulting them in parliaments and by leading them to war against France in 1492. However, the problems of the pretenders, together with increased experience of the shortcomings of the traditional systems, ended this honeymoon period.

After surviving the challenge of Perkin Warbeck and the treachery of Sir William Stanley in 1495, Henry seems to have felt utterly betrayed and to have resorted to governing with only the assistance of a handful of trusted servants. Henceforth, Henry mostly shut himself away in his Privy Chamber, where only his most trusted advisers were admitted, and his government became of necessity much more government by the household, because its officials were the only ones who had regular access to the king. This was not the beginning of a steady development in this style of government as used to be thought. Research into the Yorkist period has shown that Henry VII was merely reverting to recent practice. Moreover, it is now generally agreed, that was this practice was not continued during the reign of Henry VIII.

New age?

So the old argument that the reign of Henry VII began a 'new' age in English history has been discredited by the evidence that so many of the first Tudor's methods were similar to those of his Yorkist predecessors. It has been replaced by the judgement that, although Henry was essentially a medieval monarch, he was an outstanding example of his kind. No other king was so personally involved in matters of state, so efficient in his attention to the details of paperwork or so demanding in the high expectations he had of those who served him.

Humanism and the New Learning

However, it should not be imagined that Henry had nothing of the 'modern' in him. His reign coincided with the spread of the Renaissance northwards and there is evidence that its spirit had some effect upon him. Certainly, he was prepared to consider exploiting the new ideas and the possibilities for change that Renaissance thinking encouraged, rather than just being content to do things as they had always been done. He was farsighted enough to foster good relations with the newly united kingdom of Spain, realising the potential offered by the friendship in any struggle with the might of France. His patronage of the Cabots displayed his understanding of the advantages that exploration outside Europe was already yielding to Portugal and Spain. He

Key question
How important was humanism and the New Learning to Henry?

was aware of the financial benefits to be gained from any expansion of overseas trade and pursued this as far as his dynastic concerns allowed.

The developments in art and architecture were slow to reach England, but this did not prevent the king from commissioning new buildings: the Henry VII Chapel in Westminster Abbey, the nave at St George's Chapel in Windsor, Christchurch Gate at Canterbury, and a new palace at Richmond. Built in the Gothic style, these and many others were (and most still are) visible reminders of Tudor power, emblazoned with the family emblem, the Tudor rose. Henry used his buildings to display his importance and to remind all his subjects that he was their master. It is perhaps symbolic that his tomb, in his Memorial Chapel in Westminster Abbey where he lies with his queen, Elizabeth of York, embodies the new styles as sculpted by the Italian, Pietro Torrigiano, in the Florentine fashion. Like his

Henry VII's Memorial Chapel in Westminster Abbey. This was designed to provide a magnificent setting for the tombs of Henry and his wife. The chapel was meant to be seen as a resting place fit for a great king.

reign, his tomb was essentially medieval but with hints of a more flamboyant spirit that would flourish after his death.

Contrary to Henry's reputation for being mean with money, the expensively designed tomb effigies of himself and his wife show how prepared the king was to spend lavishly on himself and his family.

3 | Henry's Legacy: Did He Achieve His Aims?

In April 1509 Henry died suddenly from a stroke. His hard work and determination to succeed had meant that he had achieved more than any of his immediate predecessors. He had brought to an end the dynastic squabbles that had for so long rendered the monarchy a pawn of the nobility. He had overcome all potential rivals to his throne, curbed the greater magnates and restored the finances of the crown. Sadly, all this had won him respect rather than popularity. Few mourned his death. Instead, all attention was focused on his son, the new young king. Sir Thomas More spoke for many when he wrote: 'This day is the end of our slavery, the fount of our liberty; the end of sadness, the beginning of joy.' Yet with hindsight, the memorable achievements of the later Tudors were only possible because of the secure foundations laid by Henry VII.

Tomb of Henry VII and Elizabeth

Summary diagram: Henry's legacy

BALANCE SHEET			
Aims and policies	Success	Failure	Comment
Establishing the dynasty	Henry firmly established the Tudor dynasty. He defeated his rivals and the pretenders, and he secured the throne. The fact that he stayed in power and passed on his throne to his son is an impressive achievement. (First monarch to do so successfully for nearly a century.)	Henry failed to establish a sense of security. His position as king was constantly under threat until at least the last three years of his reign.	It has been argued that this was Henry's only achievement.
Finance	Henry left the crown solvent. He was the first king to do so in more than a century. The crown's finances were more stable and secure, and the methods of collection were more efficient.	Henry failed to innovate or improve upon the financial achievements of his Yorkist predecessors. The wealth amassed in his final years was by illegal or highly dubious means. The efficiency of his tax collecting methods made the king unpopular.	It has been argued that solvency was not such an achievement. No other Tudor monarch died solvent yet their reputations have not suffered as a result.
Nobility	Henry re-established the crown's primacy over the nobility. He kept the nobility in check and largely reduced the threat they posed by such devices as bonds and recognisances.	He bullied the majority of the nobility into subjection. His harsh methods were resented by many and pushed some into rebellion, e.g. Earl of Lincoln.	Had he worked more on a basis of consensus rather than coercion, he might have avoided rebellion and encouraged loyalty.
Foreign policy	He won respect for England abroad and created a stable diplomatic environment. The alliance with Spain was perhaps his greatest achievement.	He failed to play a full part in international relations. His reliance on Spain did little to enhance his dealings with other nations. By 1509 England was largely isolated.	Henry did not take advantage of his wife's death to marry a foreign princess. In human terms this was commendable but in policy terms it was a missed opportunity.
Law and order	He re-established respect for the law and restored confidence in the government after the uncertainties of the Wars of the Roses.	He failed to reduce the tension that existed between rival noble families. He failed to stop rebellions and periodic disorder from breaking out.	England was a more peaceful and stable country under Henry than it had been under the Yorkists.
The economy	Henry encouraged trade and commerce. Royal patronage, peace at home and a more stable international situation promoted economic growth.	Economic advantages were often sacrificed for gains in foreign policy.	England had become a richer country under Henry.

Further Reading

There are innumerable books available on the Tudor period that cover the reign of Henry VII. However, as the time that you will have available for additional study on the topic will probably be very limited, it will be important that you are consciously selective in your choice of further reading. Below is a list of the most useful and accessible books currently in print and available.

The following books have been written with sixth-formers and undergraduate students very much in mind:

I. Arthurson, *Documents of the Reign of Henry VII* (Cambridge Local Examinations Syndicate, 1984).

S. Doran, *England and Europe, 1485–1603* (Longman Seminar Studies, 1986).

A. Grant, *Henry VII* (Methuen, 1985).

J. Hunt and C. Towle, *Henry VII* (Longman History in Depth, 1998)

R. Lockyer and A. Thrush, *Henry VII*, 3rd edn (Longman Seminar Studies, 1997).

C. Pendrill, *The Wars of the Roses and Henry VII: England c.1459–c.1513* (Heinemann, 2004).

D. Rogerson, S. Ellsmore and D. Hudson, *The Early Tudors: England 1485–1558* (John Murray, 2001).

Glossary

Act of Resumption   An act whereby the king takes back land granted as rewards by previous monarchs.

Annex   To take over or to take control of.

Arable farming   Crop growing.

Arbitrary and authoritarian rule   The strict rule of a king who demands absolute obedience and who can make decisions without consulting anyone.

Attainder   Act of parliament registering a person's conviction for treason and declaring all his property forfeit to the king.

Auditors   Financial officials who counted and wrote down the figures in an account book.

Benevolence   A type of forced loan that would not be repaid.

Betrothal   Promise of marriage made between parents on behalf of their children.

Black Death   The plague that spread across the British Isles between 1347 and 1351 killing up to half of the population.

Casual labour   Irregularly employed workers who might be taken on seasonally.

Chamberlain of the King's Household   Official in charge of the king's household servants.

Chief Justice   Chief Judge in the king's law court.

Christopher Columbus   Italian explorer who discovered America for Spain in 1492.

Commissioners   Officials appointed by the crown to deal with specific tasks or duties.

Common law courts   Local courts in which cases involving the gentry and peasantry were heard.

Constitution   Set of rules by which a country or state is run.

Convocation   A kind of parliament for the Church in which representatives of the clergy met to discuss clerical matters.

Corporations   Traders and merchants who came together to form an organisation to promote their rights and interests.

Council   Ruling council of the king, mainly composed of his most influential nobles and gentry.

Customs duties   Taxes imposed on imported goods.

Depose   To rid the kingdom of its king by forcing him to resign.

Diocese   Territory and churches over which a bishop has control.

Doctrine   The rules, principles and teachings of the Church.

Dowry   Money or property paid by the bride's father on his daughter's marriage.

Duchy   Name given to territory ruled over by a duke.

Dynasty   A ruling family that survives for more than a single generation.

Engrossing   Where two or more farms combined to make a more economic unit.

Escheat   Where a landholder died without heirs, his lands passed by right to the king.

Eulogy   Something written in praise of a person.

Excommunicate   To cast out of or exclude from the Church.

Expansionist policy   French kings were determined to extend the borders of their kingdom to make France larger and more powerful.

Factions   Rival or opposing political groups led by powerful noblemen or noble families.

Feudal/feudalism   Terms used to describe the medieval social and political known as the feudal system.

Feudal system   A term used to describe the political and social system of medieval England. It was developed in England by William the Conqueror after the Norman Conquest as a way of controlling his new kingdom. It was based on the relationship between lord (master) and vassal (servant): in a ceremony known as homage the vassal promised to serve his lord in war and peace in return for land. This land was held with the permission of the lord who offered his vassal support and protection. The most important lord was the king and his vassals were his nobles. The nobles were lords to their vassals, the knights.

Feudatories   Semi-independent territories with feudal lords who owed nominal (in name only) allegiance to the king of France, e.g. Burgundy and Normandy.

First degree of affinity   Close relation, usually first cousins.

Gentlemen of the Bedchamber, grooms and ushers   Titles given to the personal servants of the king. Those who attended him every day.

Gentry   Class of landowners below the nobility but above the peasantry. They were divided into three social groups: knights, esquires and gentlemen.

Great Chain of Being   The belief that every man and woman was born to a specific place in the strict hierarchy of society and had a duty to remain there.

Great Chamberlain   Chief official responsible for the running of the king's household.

Great Seal   Only documents and orders bearing the great seal were lawful and could be enforced.

Habsburg Empire   Territories ruled over by the Habsburg royal family. These included Austria, parts of Germany, Italy, the Netherlands and eventually Spain.

Hanseatic League   A league of German towns which dominated trade in the Baltic and which jealously guarded its monopoly of trade there.

Heretic   Christian who denies the authority of the Church and rejects or accepts only some of its teachings.

High infant mortality   Phrase used to describe the high percentage of deaths suffered by children under the age of five.

Holy Roman Emperor   Title given to ruler of territory now occupied by modern-day Germany.

Hundred Years War   Term applied by historians to describe the state of war that existed between England and France between 1338 and 1453.

Indenture of retainder   Agreement or contract binding a servant to a master.

Indicted   Legal term used to describe those charged with a crime.

Laity   The main body of Church members who do not belong to the clergy.

Levies   Money raised by order of the king.

Lieutenancy   An official position held by a person appointed and trusted by the king to act in his name.

Live of their own   Kings were expected to live within their financial means.

Livery   The giving of a uniform or badge to a follower.

Lollardy   A heretic movement that supported the translation of the Bible into English from Latin.

Lord Protector   Title sometimes given to a regent.

Lords spiritual and temporal Terms used to describe high-ranking churchmen like bishops (lords spiritual) and the nobility like earls and dukes.

Magnates The higher or more powerful nobility usually with the rank of marquis and duke.

Maintenance The protection of a follower's interests.

Marcher lordships Territories conquered from the Welsh between 1066 and 1282 and held as personal property by the English lords who captured them. By the beginning of Henry VII's reign they numbered about 50 lordships located along the south coast of Wales and on either side of the modern boundary between England and Wales.

Marriage The royal right to arrange the marriage, for a fee, of heirs and heiresses.

Master craftsmen Skilled workers at the top of their trade.

Merchant Staplers Guild or union of merchants concerned with the export of raw wool.

Merchant Taylors Guild or union of merchants concerned with the cloth trade.

Minority rule A period when the ruler is a child or minor.

Moors of Granada Non-Christian inhabitants of Spain and Portugal. They were descendants of Muslim settlers who came from north Africa in the tenth century.

New World Term applied to the American continent and associated Caribbean islands recently discovered by Columbus.

Nobility Wealthy and powerful landowners and office holders with titles such as baron, earl, viscount, marquis and duke.

Order of the Garter An honour was bestowed on the most important knights who became the most senior rank of knighthood.

Orthodox Accepting without question the doctrine of the Church.

Overlordship One person having power over another or over his lands such as a lord over his vassal.

Papal dispensation The written permission of the Pope enabling a ruling monarch to marry or divorce.

Papal tax collector Official appointed by the Pope in Rome to collect revenue owed to the Church in countries such as England.

Pastoral duties The duty of care exercised by a priest to his parishioners such as baptism, marriage and burial.

Pasture farming Animal rearing.

Patronage The award and distribution of royal favours.

Paupers and vagrants The very poor who had no homes and were left to wander from place to place to beg.

Plantagenets Name given to the ruling family of England at that time.

Pluralism The holding of more than one parish by a clergyman.

Poll tax Tax imposed on individual people.

Prerogative rights The rights and privileges held by the monarchy such as the right to tax, lead the nation in war and dispense justice.

Privy seal King's personal seal, made from metal and pressed into wax. It was a substitute for his signature and was used to authenticate documents.

Propaganda Method by which ideas are spread to support a particular point of view.

Quasi-kings Nobles behaving as kings in their own lordships with the power to make laws, impose and collect taxes and erect castles.

Receivers Financial officials who collected and stored money on behalf of the king.

Re-endowment Re-investment, or finding other ways of raising money for the crown.

Regent Someone who governs the kingdom on behalf of a king.

Regular clergy Monks and nuns who devoted their lives to prayer and study in monasteries. They tended to keep themselves sheltered from the outside world.

Relief A payment the king received on the transfer of lands through inheritance.

Renaissance A rebirth of learning and the arts, which encouraged writers and artists to become part of what was called the spirit of New Learning.

Retainers A small, permanent professional force of trained soldiers who wore the uniform of the lords they served either for pay or for land.

Retrenchment Cutting down on expenditure.

Royal Commissioners Local officials directly appointed by the king to see to his affairs.

Sanctuary The Church offered protection from the law for up to 40 days but, by the fifteenth century, sanctuaries in major towns were sheltering people for indefinite periods, although this was a source of dispute with some kings.

Secular clergy Parish priests, chaplains and bishops who lived in the outside world. They performed tasks such as marriage, baptism and burial.

Selective breeding Ensuring that only the most healthy animals were allowed to breed to strengthen the blood-line.

Serfdom A medieval social and economic system whereby peasants are tied to the land on which they live and work.

Service nobility Nobles created by the king to serve the crown.

Simony The selling of church appointments.

Solvent Financially sound and without debt.

Staple Company concerned with the export of raw wool.

Subsidy A grant of money made by parliament to the king usually for a specific purpose.

Tariff Tax on imported goods.

Trade embargo A country's refusal to trade with another.

Treason Betrayal of one's country and its ruler.

Treasurer of the Chamber Chief financial official responsible for the king's money.

Treasury Held the king's wealth in money and goods.

Usurpation Where the throne is seized without authority or in opposition to the rightful line of succession.

Vagabondage To be landless and unemployed.

Wardship A lord's duty of care for the upbringing, education and marriage of the under-age children of dead vassals, and looking after their lands until they reach adulthood.

Wars of the Roses First used in the nineteenth century to describe the sequence of plots, rebellions and battles that took place between 1455 and 1485. The idea of the warring roses of Lancaster (red) and York (white) was invented by Henry VII after he seized the throne in 1485.

Index